D1408428

HORIZON

MAY, 1961 · VOLUME III, NUMBER 5

© 1961 by American Horizon, Inc. All rights reserved under Berne and Pan-American Copyright Conventions. Reproduction in whole or in part of any article without permission is prohibited. U. S. copyright is not claimed for the color plates appearing on pages 6–7, 10–11, 14–15, 20, 23, 24–25, 31, 78–79.
Printed in the United States of America.

COURTESY *Connaissance des Arts*

HORIZON

MAY, 1961 • VOLUME III, NUMBER 5

PUBLISHER
James Parton

EDITOR
Joseph J. Thorndike, Jr.

MANAGING EDITOR
William Harlan Hale

ASSOCIATE EDITORS
Ralph Backlund
Robert Emmett Ginna

ASSISTANT EDITORS
Ada Pesin
Jane Wilson

CONTRIBUTING EDITOR
Margery Darrell

EDITORIAL ASSISTANTS
Shirley Abbott, Caroline Backlund,
Wendy Buehr, Alan Doré

COPY EDITOR
Mary Ann Pfeiffer
Assistants: Rita Resnikoff, Ruth H. Wolfe

ART DIRECTOR
Irwin Glusker
Associate Art Director: Elton Robinson

ADVISORY BOARD
Gilbert Highet, *Chairman*
Frederick Burkhardt, Oliver Jensen
Marshall B. Davidson, Jotham Johnson
Richard M. Ketchum, John Walker

EUROPEAN CONSULTING EDITOR
J. H. Plumb
Christ's College, Cambridge

EUROPEAN BUREAU
Gertrudis Feliu, *Chief*
28 Quai du Louvre, Paris

CIRCULATION DIRECTOR
Richard V. Benson

HORIZON is published every two months by American Horizon, Inc., a subsidiary of American Heritage Publishing Co., Inc. Executive and editorial offices: 551 Fifth Ave., New York 17, N.Y. HORIZON welcomes contributions but can assume no responsibility for unsolicited material.

All correspondence about subscriptions should be addressed to: HORIZON Subscription Office, 383 West Center St., Marion, Ohio.

Single Copies: $4.50
Annual Subscriptions: $21.00 in the U.S. & Can.
$22.00 elsewhere

An annual index is published every September, priced at $1. HORIZON is also indexed in the *Readers Guide to Periodical Literature.*

Title registered U.S. Patent Office
Second-class postage paid at New York, N.Y.

COVER: Eugène Delacroix was never more in his element of violent drama and intense color than when painting his *Abduction of Rebecca* (1846), a masterly canvas inspired by Sir Walter Scott's romance *Ivanhoe* and that now hangs in the Metropolitan Museum of Art. Here the heroine, Rebecca, is seen at the moment when, amid the siege of the burning castle of Torquilstone in which she has been held prisoner, she is seized by the African slaves of the Templar Bois-Guilbert (at right) who has evil designs on her. A survey of "The Romantic Revolt," including Delacroix's place in it, begins on page 58.

FRONTISPIECE: The artists of the Baroque age spent a great deal of time turning natural objects—rocks, shells, ostrich eggs—into something else. This resplendent cup is an example of what they could do with a pearly nautilus shell. The shells, brought to Europe by voyagers to the Indian Ocean and beyond, were transformed into fantastic swans, ships, sea monsters—but most often cups (purely ornamental: What vintage could measure up?). They were much admired by German princes and Dutch burghers who used them to dress their sideboards. This cup, mounted in silver gilt, was probably made by an Italian goldsmith in the first half of the sixteenth century, when the vogue was just getting under way. It is now in the Lázaro Galdiano Museum in Madrid.

THE

Its skies are still spacious, its purple mountains still majestic—but the

No people has inherited a more naturally beautiful land than we: within an area representing a mere 6 per cent of the land surface of the globe we in America can point to mountain ranges as spectacular as those of the Dolomites and to tropical jungles as colorful as those of the Amazon valley; to lake-studded forests as lovely as those of Finland and to rolling hills as gentle as those around Salzburg; to cliffs that rival those of the French Riviera and to sandy beaches that are unexcelled even by those along the shores of Jutland; in short, to about as varied and thrilling a geography as has ever been presented to man.

The only trouble is that we are about to turn this beautiful heritage into the biggest slum on the face of the earth. "The mess that is man-made America," as a British magazine has called it, is a disgrace of such vast proportions that only a concerted national effort can now hope to return physical America to the community of civilized nations.

Our towns and cities boast many isolated handsome buildings—but very, very few handsome streets, squares, civic centers, or neighborhoods. (Even such rare exceptions as Rockefeller Center in New York, now twenty-five years old, have become disfigured as they expand beyond their original limits.) Our suburbs are interminable wastelands dotted with millions of monotonous little houses on monotonous little lots and crisscrossed by highways lined with billboards, jazzed-up diners, used-car lots, drive-in movies, beflagged gas stations, and garish motels. Even the relatively unspoiled countryside beyond these suburban fringes has begun to sprout more telephone poles than trees, more bowling alleys than latter-day "Oak Alleys," more trailer camps than national parks. And the shores of oceans, lakes, and rivers are rapidly becoming encrusted with the junkiness of industries that pollute the water on which they feed.

Let us face it: Where in America is there a waterfront as handsome as that of Copenhagen? (That of Chicago is virtually cut off from the city proper by multi-lane highways crossed only in a very few places by pedestrian bridges.) Where in America is there an urban riverbank as lovely as that of the Seine in Paris? (Admittedly, they have recently built a sunken motor highway along one bank of the Seine, but at least it is *sunken*—in vivid contrast to the situation in Providence, Rhode Island, where most of the river has been paved over to provide space for automobiles.) And where in America is there a harbor as lively and exciting as the Vieux Port in Marseilles? (New Yorkers are *told* by foreigners that theirs is a port city, but unless they take an occasional hazardous glimpse from the elevated West Side Highway—which effectively conceals New York's harbor from the eyes of pedestrians—they have no way of verifying this claim.) As for our suburbs and exploited countrysides, the less said the better. We do have many superhighways that enable us to traverse these scenic spots at maximum speeds—but, alas, the attainable speeds are not always quite maximum enough.

Most of us know most of this to be true, but not all of us are greatly concerned about it. When foreign and domestic critics of man-made America blame "the authorities" for not protecting the natural resources of the American landscape and townscape, they ignore the fact that "the authorities" have only as much authority as the voters are willing to grant them. And when more sophisticated critics blame certain pressure groups for denying such authority to planning commissions and the like, they ignore the fact that pressure groups for special interests, such as the billboard industry, are effective only when the majority of the voters simply don't care enough.

The majority of Americans (and the majority of the inhabitants of most other industrialized nations) are, indeed, fairly indifferent to the issue of beauty. The mess created

UGLY AMERICA

·ruited plain is becoming an eyesore from sea to shining sea *By* PETER BLAKE

along the fringes of our suburban highways is not the work of some numerically small and diabolical pressure group but, rather, the work of hundreds of thousands of "average citizens"—shopkeepers, gas-station owners, hot-dog vendors, and the like. Throughout rural America a new generation of farmers is befouling the face of its inherited land with a new growth of tin cans, big and small: trailers, silos, storage tanks, prefab sheds, and just plain, ordinary oil drums. These are people of goodwill, not money-mad lobbyists. Why, then, do they behave like vandals?

There are two principal reasons: the first is that most of us have, in effect, lost the discriminating use of our eyes. Every teacher in the visual arts knows that his most difficult task is to make his students see things again. Most of us have lost all appreciation of color, and much the same is true of our appreciation of everyday objects: a rose is no longer a rose, with a quality of its own, so much as a symbol of something else—like spring, or love, or whiskey. The constant impact of screaming colors, posters, and "spectaculars" dulls our sense of discrimination and other senses as well.

The second reason why most of us behave like vandals is that ours has become a throw-away civilization: it sometimes seems as if almost everything we own has been designed, carefully and deliberately, to fall apart at the earliest possible moment in order to induce us to buy a replacement. The concept of "lasting values"—in the area of our physical belongings, at any rate—has almost completely vanished.

Indeed, universal vandalism has become public policy. Ogden Nash may have thought that he was exaggerating when he wrote:

I think that I shall never see
A billboard lovely as a tree.
Perhaps, unless the billboards fall,
I'll never see a tree at all.

But the fact of the matter is that in Chicago, for example, the city authorities have been busy cutting down the tops of any trees that interfere with the view of billboards along Lake Shore Drive. On the other hand, any suburban developer who plants new trees between his houses (to conceal the freshly planted telephone poles) will find that the United States government, through its Federal Housing Administration appraisers, gives him virtually no credit for his efforts —which means, in effect, that he must pay for those trees out of his own pocket. At the same time, however, the government *will* give him credit (about $300 per house, if his houses sell for $20,000) for "sales promotion"—a large part of which consists of defacing the landscape with hideously garlanded model houses, billboards, and side shows along the nearest highway. In short, it is the policy of at least one agency of the Federal government to reward those who desecrate America and to penalize those who wish to beautify it.

Needless to say, there are quite a few powerful and well-organized pressure groups that have a vested interest in the desecration of America. The billboard industry is one of these. Around San Francisco, for example, the industry has almost succeeded in blocking the view from most highways of one of the loveliest cities in the world—and one of the most beautiful bays. A rare exception is a short stretch of the Redwood Highway which leads from San Francisco to Sausalito: this stretch happens to pass through some hills owned by the Federal government, and the billboard boys have so far failed to plant their standards on those hills. But they have more than made up for this failure elsewhere: to the north, in Seattle—a city that once boasted of some of the most beautiful environs in the world—the billboards have successfully blocked out nature; and to the south, in the region around Los Angeles, billboards have even become air-borne to plaster their messages—on streamers—all over the sky.

Three years ago, when the Federal Highways Program was

TEXT CONTINUED ON PAGE 18

I will build a motor car for the great multitude. . . . But it will be so low in price that no man making a good salary will be unable to own one—and enjoy with his family the blessing of hours of pleasure in God's great open spaces.

HENRY FORD

HERBERT LOEBEL

NO
STANDING
BUS STOP
ESSO
Valiant
WURTZ
LYMOUTH
PUBLIC TELEPHONE
OFFICIAL
STATE OF NEW YORK
MOTOR VEHICLE
INSPECTION STATION
YIELD
to
Pedestrians
in Crosswalks
WURTZEL SERVICE CENTER
FREE INSPECTION
WE LINE-UP
and
BALANCE
COMPLETE
AUTO
REPAIRS
MECHANIC
ON DUTY
BODY WORK

Often I think of the beautiful town
That is seated by the sea;
Often in thought go up and down
The pleasant streets of that dear old town,
And my youth comes back to me.

HENRY WADSWORTH LONGFELLOW

HERBERT LOEBEL

OFFICE
VILLAGE
E 104 ST

Westward the course of empire takes its way;

The four first Acts already past,

A fifth shall close the Drama with the day;

Time's noblest offspring is the last.

GEORGE BERKELEY

WILLIAM A. GARNETT

INSCRIPTION FOR THE ENTRANCE TO A WOOD

. . . enter this wild wood

And view the haunts of Nature. The calm shade

Shall bring a kindred calm; and the sweet breeze

That makes the green leaves dance, shall waft a balm

To thy sick heart. Thou wilt find nothing here

Of all that pained thee in the haunts of man

And made thee loathe thy life.

WILLIAM CULLEN BRYANT

FREE LANCE PHOTOGRAPHERS GUILD

NO
DUMPING
ALLOWED

And may we not also hope that the day will arrive when the improvements and comforts to social life shall spread over the vast area of this continent?

HENRY CLAY

HERBERT LOEBEL

Thank God, men cannot as yet fly, and lay waste the sky as well as the earth!

HENRY DAVID THOREAU

LLOYD SHEARER—EXPRESS NEWS & FEATURES SERVICE

TEXT CONTINUED FROM PAGE 5
being discussed in Congress, newspapers and magazines all over the United States argued in favor of amendments that would have banned billboards from the new highways. This campaign called for considerable courage, for the billboard lobby is supported by the same advertisers who keep magazines and newspapers solvent. Alas, the outcome was a sad compromise: it was left to the states to decide what restrictions, if any, should be placed on the billboard industry. Since most state legislatures become notoriously flexible when confronted with well-heeled lobbyists, the "compromise" was really a victory for Madison Avenue. Still, the public *was* aroused to a degree and might well have been persuaded to demand effective controls. Yet the opportunity was missed. When asked at a press conference what he planned to do about the matter, President Eisenhower said, "I am against those billboards that mar our scenery, [but] I don't know what I can do about it." Another man of goodwill—and an amateur artist to boot—but seemingly helpless to stem the tide.

The issue of aesthetic control is no different from any other that involves certain controls over sectors of the economy. In other areas we have had to prohibit activities that adversely affect the freedom, health, or safety of the average citizen. The drug industry can sell good or indifferent drugs, but it may not poison its customers; Detroit can make any car its heart desires, but the car must be safe to drive; airlines and railroads are rigidly controlled to protect their passengers' lives. Only the honky-tonk business (with some of its related businessmen) seems exempt. The reasons most frequently given are two: first, it is said that aesthetic vandalism does not adversely affect the freedom, health, or safety of the average citizen. This is nonsense, as we shall see in a moment. And secondly, it is said that "you cannot legislate beauty." This is true. But you *can* legislate order, and we know that without order there is no real hope for beauty.

Robert Moses, who knows a good deal about highways, has stated unequivocally that eyesores along our roads are traffic hazards. During the great Congressional billboard battle in the spring of 1958, Moses cited a study made several years earlier by the Minnesota Department of Highways which indicated quite clearly that accident rates are related to the frequency of roadside signs. Unfortunately, many of the victims of such accidents can no longer testify to the truth of this observation; but any living motorist knows how distracting billboards and other roadside clutter can be, especially at night. In other words, billboards do adversely affect the health and safety of the average citizen just as surely as do impure foods and drugs.

Regarding the question of whether or not beauty can be legislated, the Supreme Court has made its position clear: "The concept of the public welfare is broad and inclusive," it stated in a decision not long ago. "The values [the public welfare] represents are spiritual as well as physical, aesthetic as well as monetary. It is within the power of the legislature to determine that the community should be beautiful as well as healthy. . . ." Most architects, artists, and planners might feel that the Supreme Court went pretty far out on a limb that time. (Who is to decide what is beautiful and what is not?) Still, if the Supreme Court thinks that beauty can be legislated, it would certainly agree that the prerequisite for beauty, namely order, can and must be legislated. After all, "order" is what society is all about.

The most widely accepted instrument of planning in the United States is zoning. It is a rather negative, or back-door, approach to planning (because "planning" is a dirty word in many parts of America), but it is at least a first step.

What a zoning law sets forth, in effect, is what you can *not* do to a given piece of land that you own. It may say that you can not use it for anything but residential or industrial or commercial or institutional structures (or a mixture of two or three of these); it may say that you can not overbuild—too high, or too close to front and side lines of the property; it may say that you can not park your cars or trucks in the public street—that you must provide off-street parking and loading; and so on. But zoning stops far short of the Supreme Court's suggestion that beauty should be legislated; zoning merely outlaws chaos.

In spite of this, all hell breaks loose every time a community tries to introduce more stringent zoning laws. In some very important cities there is no zoning law to this day: in Houston, Texas, the sixth largest in America, zoning has been fought passionately and successfully for years by a small and immensely wealthy group—whose members, oddly enough, all live in a delightful suburban enclave called River Oaks, which is just about the most rigidly controlled and most rigidly zoned community anywhere in the United States. Meanwhile, the poor unzoned citizenry that cannot afford to live in River Oaks (or happens to have picked the wrong ancestors) resides and works in a town so chaotic that a single block may boast a ranch house on one corner, a junk yard next to it, a funeral parlor next to *that*, a bowling alley next to the funeral parlor, then another ranch house, and, finally, an iridescent billboard telling you how to get away from it all by TWA. There may be some exaggeration here, but not much.

In fact, the only kind of "zoning" that exists in a city like Houston is that brought about unintentionally by vast suburban developments consisting of house after house after house after house. And this type of "suburban sprawl" is, of course, one of the most offensive sights and blights of all on the American scene. Zoning is almost wholly ineffective in combating such sprawl; indeed, some standard zoning laws have actually aggravated it by insisting upon meaningless setbacks of houses from side lines and sidewalks.

The vital statistics of suburban sprawl are terrifying: there is the fact that, today, some 50 million Americans live in these suburban developments and that, within twenty years, another 50 million are expected to move into them;

there is the further fact that since World War II, about five million acres of our countryside have been covered with little houses on little lots (and the services that go with this). And here are some detailed statistics: Nassau County, New York, which is almost entirely suburban, grew from a population of 672,765 in 1950 to 1,300,171 in 1960—which means that in this one county alone some 90,000 additional acres have been swallowed up—almost half the county's land. Irving, Texas, a suburban community near Dallas, grew from 2,621 inhabitants in 1950 to 45,985 in 1960—all of them suburbanites, all spread out over some 13,000 acres of newly developed land (and the town is trying to annex another 60,000 acres for additional suburban development). Orange County, in California, which forms a large chunk of Los Angeles' suburbia, more than tripled its population between 1950 and 1960. Phoenix, Arizona, moved up from being the ninety-eighth city in the United States in 1950 to the twenty-ninth in 1960—almost all the growth taking place in vast suburban developments that now cover the once beautiful desert like some dreadful skin cancer.

There is not much that we can do about the population explosion that lies at the base of all this; but there *is* something we should have done long ago about the pattern of housing this exploding population. For the suburban pattern that has developed in the United States—and is being encouraged by mortgage bankers and the government's F.H.A. policies—not only eats up land at a prolific rate but is bankrupting most suburbs and is, further, making life there only slightly less intolerable than on tenement streets.

The mess that is suburban America starts with the sentimental assumption that everybody should live in a detached house on a small lot. The most common residential "unit" today is a single house of about 1,000 square feet placed on a lot that is 60 feet wide along the street and about 120 feet deep. The house is set back some 25 feet from the sidewalk and about 10 feet from each of the side lines of the property. Because the owners have but limited resources of time and money, they often improve only that part of their lot which represents their "front" to the outside world. These front yards are, of course, unusable for outdoor living because common restrictions against fences rob them of all privacy. The rear yard is frequently neglected, and in any case, it is not really big enough for growing children to play in. So the children play in the street; the parents spend most of their time on maintaining a front garden which they can't use; the community has to maintain long roads and long utility lines to service its strung-out houses; and the suburbs go broke.

There is a better way. It is entirely possible to build 1,000-square-foot, two-story houses on lots that measure only 20 feet wide by 50 feet deep. Such houses would be attached to one another, yet staggered so that each would have a completely private patio space of its own, big enough for large outdoor parties and small enough for any family to maintain without trouble. The "surplus land" thus saved—something like 6,000 square feet per family—could then be pooled to create several large communal parks and playgrounds, each big enough for ball games, etc., each maintained by a small annual contribution from member families. (It is much cheaper to maintain a single large park than a dozen small gardens; and it is much cheaper for a builder to bypass a hilly and wooded site than to flatten it with bulldozers and to cut down all its trees.) This sort of plan not only preserves much of the natural beauty of the areas that surround our cities but also reduces the cost of roads and utilities and, thus, the suburban tax-burden.

None of this is theory: it has been practiced for years in every Western country including, occasionally, the United States. Baldwin Hills, in Los Angeles, was built twenty years ago along the lines described above; today it is the most desirable middle-income community in Southern California.

So the wholesale destruction of our countryside is not the inevitable result of the population explosion. It is the result of incompetence and ignorance on the part of those who determine the shape of our suburbs. And it is also the result of pressures from those who speculate with land and who have a vested interest in making buildable land scarce and, thus, increasingly valuable. Under the present system of suburban development, the land speculator has been able to make phenomenal profits: between 1950 and 1960, while the Consumer Price Index went up just a little more than 10 per cent, the price of suburban land rose anywhere from 100 to 3,760 per cent, and the end is nowhere in sight.

Yet even if we managed to arrest suburban sprawl and managed to outlaw honky-tonks, we would not necessarily create a beautiful man-made America. All we might hope to get is a kind of city and a kind of suburb in which beauty is *possible*—which is a good deal more than we have now.

The achievement of beauty is a creative act, and it is quite possible that we are not at present capable of performing such a one. But we are capable of creating order, and we have demonstrated this in many sciences and even in some areas of political science. If the cities that men build and leave behind them reflect the level of a civilization, then our civilization deserves something better: Hackensack really is not a true image of our time.

Just how much better we can do depends, to a large extent, upon how much we learn to care—upon how lividly angry we can get at the vulgarians who are befouling our land to make a fast buck faster. The time is long overdue for Americans to become outraged at the things that are being done to our cities and countrysides in the name of our "way of life." The hour has come to outlaw barbarism.

Peter Blake is a practicing architect and the author of a recent book, The Master Builders, *which examines the work of Frank Lloyd Wright, Le Corbusier, and Mies van der Rohe.*

SAIDENBERG GALLERY, N.Y.

By DORE ASHTON

EASTFOTO

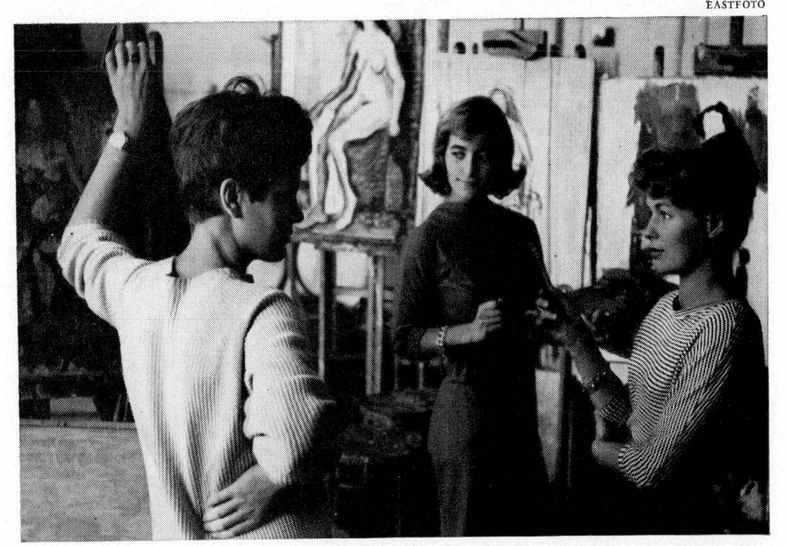

Three students talk things over at the Warsaw Academy of Fine Arts

ABOUT-FACE IN POLAND

In a youthful rebellion against stodgy formulas, Polish art has now become as adventurous as any in the world

Farmers and factory workers—long regarded as the only subject of art in Eastern Europe—have disappeared so completely from the canvases of Poland's youngest painters that they are now nearly extinct. In the past two or three years, the new generation of Polish artists has abandoned the requirements of "socialist realism" to join the international abstract confraternity—and with remarkable success. Poland's abstract painters now exhibit all over Europe and often take international prizes; they have penetrated some of the major collections of modern art in both Europe and the United States; and they will be represented in New York and Washington this spring by large gallery shows and later by a major exhibition at the Museum of Modern Art, which will then circulate throughout the country.

In Warsaw recently I asked a middle-aged professor of painting how he could account for the seemingly limitless enthusiasm of these young insurgents. "Ah," he said, "you must remember that Poles are by nature anarchists. If one thing is expected of them, you may be sure they will do the opposite." This ironic explanation is naturally oversimplified, but it does characterize the passionate course of twentieth-century Polish art history, which is fraught with eruptions, struggles, rejections, and re-formations. The first of these successive waves of avant-garde activity was influenced by the three major movements prior to World War I: futurism, cubism, and German expressionism. The next and more significant formation was the *Blok* group, established in 1924. It expounded the "purist" and geometric principles developed by the early Russian modernist Kasimir Malevich. One of its founders, Henryk Stazewski, who had worked with Malevich in Moscow, is to

Tadeusz Kantor's big, explosive Alalaha *is about as far from "socialist realism" as you can get, but it is typical of the art being produced in Poland these days. Painted in Cracow in 1958, its style clearly reflects the influence of the late Jackson Pollock, just as its slashing violence reflects the lingering anguish of Poland's wartime experience. Kantor made his first appearance on the American scene with an impressive exhibition in New York early last fall.*

SAIDENBERG GALLERY, N.Y.

WILLIAM A. SMITH

Tadeusz Kantor (at top) was the first Polish artist to go in for free-wheeling abstraction and is still the leader of the group, although Henryk Stazewski (above) is greatly revered as an earlier experimenter.

this day a revered master in Poland, though few contemporary painters are involved with purism at the moment.

In 1933 the Cracow group, still active, was organized in opposition to the conservative academy. One of its members, Tadeusz Kantor (born in 1915), is largely credited with having kept the experimental spirit alive during the Nazi occupation. He and a number of Cracow painters and writers founded a clandestine theater which, as one critic described it, "took the plastic painting rather than the word as its point of departure." Kantor's imaginative leadership continued when he became the first Polish painter to be influenced by the "informal," or "lyrical," kind of abstraction which had gained momentum in Paris and New York after the war. Later, he was reported to have introduced the "American note" in his 1956 Warsaw exhibition.

Today there are countless such "groups" in Poland. Take, for example, the Confrontation group in Warsaw, which numbers among its painters several budding international reputations. The group operates in a large four-story building provided rent-free by the state. Each month one member is given a large exhibition. The catalogue foreword is generally written by Aleksander Wojciechowski, brilliant former editor of the only art review in Poland and passionate student of the avant-garde everywhere.

Since Poland is perhaps the poorest and certainly the most terribly devastated of all the satellite countries, these artists have no possibility of commercial success on their home grounds. The only collectors in Poland are the state institutions—no one else can yet afford to buy paintings and sculpture.

But on the whole the Polish painters seem to have a privileged position. With the aid of state grants—small sums, usually, but enough to get an artist to Paris, Venice, or Vienna for a few weeks or months—nearly all of the most gifted younger painters have been able to visit other countries.

These include people like Tadeusz Brzozowski, who recently had a highly praised one-man show in Paris. Although he heads a folk-craft school in the Tatra mountains, his expressionistic abstractions are highly sophisticated. Jan Lebenstein (born in 1930) has also been warmly received in Paris, where he won an award at the 1959 Biennale. Stefan Gierowski, thirty-six, produces elegant, cool, white-gray paintings that have been affected by American trends. Bronislaw Kierzkowski, a year older, experiments with stucco, plastics, and pieces of metal in his painting-reliefs. And there is Aleksander Kobzdej, whose thicky painted, many-layered abstractions scored highly in a New York show last year.

These are only a few of the painters meriting serious appraisal. Young as they are, they are already the grand old men of the Polish artistic revolution. Nobody can tell what will happen next, but then, nobody ever could in Poland. That is one of Poland's great weaknesses and certainly one of its significant strengths.

GALERIE CHALETTE, N.Y.

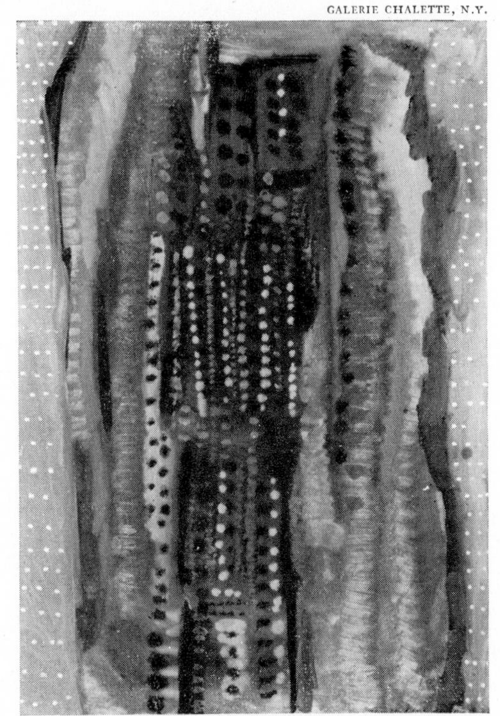

GALERIE CHALETTE, N.Y.

Although they are uniformly abstract, the new Polish artists do not all work in an angry, eruptive style. Stefan Gierowski's richly textured canvases (left) are cool, elegant, and severe. Bronislaw Kierzkowski is now painting brightly patterned gouaches (above), but he has also experimented extensively with making relieflike paintings of "new" materials. Jan Lebenstein, younger than either, paints somber, rather enigmatic images like the one below. He calls it Personnage.

JOSEPH H. HIRSHHORN COLLECTION, N.Y.

Bicyclists and strollers are silhouetted against the Persian sunset as they pass through the arcades of the Khaju bridge in Isfahan—some homeward bound, some awaiting the evening's pleasures. The rooms and pavilions under its tiled arches have been the social gathering places for noble and commoner alike ever since the Safavid Shah Abbas II built the bridge to adorn his capital three hundred years ago.

EWING KRAININ

EVENINGS AT THE BRIDGE

By TERENCE O'DONNELL

Beginning at the Colored Mountain in the Bakhtiari ranges of western Persia, the river Zayandeh Rud flows eastward beneath a score of hump-backed bridges as simple, strong, and beautiful as the deserts which surround them. But it is at the oasis and city called Isfahan that the river is cut by the piers of one of the most remarkable bridges in the world, the Khaju.

The city to which this bridge leads is equally remarkable —more than remarkable, for it is perhaps the most beautiful city in the East. A town had existed for centuries in this fertile oasis on the central Persian plateau, but it was not until the seventeenth century that Shah Abbas I chose it as his capital. Abbas, the greatest monarch of the Safavid Dynasty (1502–1736) and one of the greatest rulers in Persia's more than two thousand years of monarchy, applied his exceptional energy and taste to make his capital the fairest in the world. And according to the reports of European travel-

Stretching for one hundred and fifty-four yards, the bridge also forms a dam that can control the flow of the river beneath it.

INCE MORATH—MAGNUM

ers, it was. He built mosques and palaces, religious schools, bridges, caravansaries, promenades, and, finally, the great square which he set about with some of the most vivid—and perfect—architecture in the world.

It was a fortunate time in which to build, for the seventeenth century was a great period in Persian art. The architects, the tile and carpet makers, the potters, painters, calligraphers, and metalsmiths worked throughout Abbas's reign and those of his successors to enrich the city. Travelers entering from the desert were confounded by what must have seemed an illusion: a great garden filled with nightingales and roses, cut by canals and terraced promenades, studded with water tanks of turquoise tile in which were reflected the glistening blue curves of a hundred domes. At the heart of all of this was the square, which one such traveler declared to be "as spacious, as pleasant and aromatick a Market as any in the Universe." In time Isfahan came to be known as "half the world," Isfahan *nisf-i-jahan.*

In the early eighteenth century this fantastic city, then the size of London, started to decline. The Afghans invaded; the Safavids fell from power; the capital went elsewhere; the desert encroached. Isfahan became more of a legend than a place, and now it is for many people simply a name to which they attach their notions of old Persia and sometimes of the East. They think of it as a kind of spooky museum in which they may half see and half imagine the old splendor.

Those who actually get there find that it isn't spooky at all but as brilliant as a tile in sunlight. But even for them it remains a museum, or perhaps it would be more accurate to say a tomb, a tomb in which Persia lies well preserved but indeed dead. Everyone is ready to grant the Persians their history, but almost no one is willing to acknowledge their present. It seems that for Persia, and especially for this city, there are only two times: the glorious past and the corrupt, depressing, sterile present. The one apparent connection between the two is a score of buildings which somehow or other have survived and which naturally enough are called "historical monuments."

However, just as all the buildings have not fallen and flowed back to their original mud, so the values which wanted

EWING KRAININ

At the far ends and center of the structure are two-storied hexagonal pavilions with terraced walks and cobbled steps below.

them and saw that they were built have not all disappeared. The values and talents which made the tile and the dome, the rug, the poem and the miniature, continue in certain social institutions which rise above the ordinary life of this city, as the great buildings rise above blank walls and dirty lanes. Often, too, the social institutions are housed in these pavilions and palaces and bridges, for these great structures are not simply "historical monuments"; they are the places where Persians live.

The promenade, for example, continues to take place on the Chahar Bagh, a mile-long garden of plane and poplar trees that now serves as the city's principal street. It takes place as well along the terraces and through the arcades of the Khaju bridge, and also in the gardens of the square. On Fridays, the day when many Persians relax with poetry, talk, and a samovar, people do not, it is true, stream into Chehel Sotun—a pavilion and garden built by Shah Abbas II in the seventeenth century—but they do retire into hundreds of pavilions throughout the city and up the river valley, which are smaller, more humble copies of the former. And of course religious life continues to center in the more famous mosques, and commercial life—very much a social institution—in the bazaar. Those three other great activities of the Persians, the bath, the teahouse, and the *zur khaneh* (the latter a kind of club in which a leader and a group of men in an octagonal pit move through a rite of calisthenics, dance, chanted poetry, and music), do not take place in buildings to which entrance tickets are sold, but some of them occupy splendid examples of Persian domestic architecture: long, domed, chalk-white rooms with daises of turquoise tile, their end walls cut through to the orchards and the sky by open arches.

But more important, and the thing which the casual traveler and the blind sojourner often do not see, is that these places and activities are often the settings in which Persians exercise their extraordinary aesthetic sensibilities. Water, air, fruit, poetry, music, the human form—these things are important to Persians, and they experience them with an intense and discriminating awareness.

I should like, by the way, to make it clear that I am not

On a terrace beside the water a man kneels to pray, and for those few moments—even on the busy bridge—he is alone with Allah.

PHOTOGRAPHS EWING KRAININ

using the word "Persians" carelessly. I don't mean a few aesthetes who play about with sensations, like a young prince in a miniature dabbling his hand in a pool. These things are important to almost all Persians and perhaps most important to the most ordinary. The men crying love poems in an orchard on any summer's night are as often as not the *lutihaw*, mustachioed toughs who spend most of their lives in and out of the local prisons, brothels, and teahouses. A few months ago it was a fairly typical landlord who in the dead of night lugged me up a mountainside to drink from a spring famous in the neighborhood for its clarity and flavor. Not long ago an acquaintance, a slick-headed water rat of a lad up from the maw of the city, stood on the balcony puffing his first cigarette in weeks. The air, he said, was just right; a cigarette would taste particularly good. I really didn't know what he meant. It was a nice day, granted. But *he* knew; he sniffed the air and licked it on his lip and knew as a vintner knows a vintage.

The natural world then, plus poetry and some kinds of art, receives from the most ordinary of Persians a great deal of attention. The line of an eyebrow, the color of the skin, a ghazal from Hafiz, the purity of spring water, the long afternoon among the boughs which crowd the upper story of a pavilion—these things are noticed, judged, and valued.

Nowhere in Isfahan is this rich aesthetic life of the Persians shown so well as during the promenade at the Khaju bridge. There has probably always been a bridge of some sort at the southeastern corner of the city. For one thing, there is a natural belt of rock across the river bed; for another, it was here that one of the old caravan routes came in. It was to provide a safe and spacious crossing for these caravans, and also to make a pleasance for the city, that Shah Abbas II in about 1657 built, of sun-baked brick, tile, and stone, the present bridge. It is a splendid structure. From upstream it looks like a long arcaded box laid across the river; from downstream, where the water level is much lower, it is a high, elaborately façaded pavilion.

The top story contains more than thirty alcoves separated from each other by spandrels of blue and yellow tile. At either end and in the center there are bays which contain nine

Two of the pleasures of the bridge are food and conversation. The lion may have once marked a hero's grave in a nearby cemetery.

greater alcoves as frescoed and capacious as church apses. Here, in the old days—when they had come to see the moon or displays of fireworks—sat the king and his court while priests, soldiers, and other members of the party lounged in the smaller alcoves between.

Below, twenty vaults tunnel through the understructure of the bridge. These are traversed by another line of vaults, and thus rooms, arched on all four sides, are formed. Down through the axis of the bridge there is a long diminishing vista like a visual echo of piers and arches, while the vaults fronting upstream and down frame the sunset and sunrise, the mountains and river pools. Here, on the hottest day, it is cool beneath the stone and fresh from the water flowing in the sluices at the bottom of the vaults.

On the downstream, or "pavilion," side these vaults give out onto terraces twice as wide as the bridge itself. From the terraces—eighteen in all—broad flights of steps descend into the water or onto still more terraces barely above the level of the river. Out of water, brick, and tile they have made far more than just a bridge.

On spring and summer evenings people leave their shops and houses and walk up through the lanes of the city to the bridge. It is a great spectacle. The bridge itself rises up from the river, light-flared and enormous, like the outdoor set for an epic opera. Crowds press along the terraces, down the steps, in and out of the arcades, massing against it as though it were a fortress under siege. All kinds come to walk in the promenade: merchants from the bazaar bickering over a deal; a Bakhtiari khan in a cap and hacking jacket; dervishes who stand with the stillness of the blind, their eyes filmed with rheum and visions; the old Kajar princes arriving in their ancient limousines; students, civil servants, beggars, musicians, hawkers, and clowns. Families go out to the edge of the terraces to sit on carpets around a samovar. Below, people line the steps, as though on bleachers, to watch the sky and river. Above, in the tiled prosceniums of the alcoves, boys sing the ghazals of Hafiz and Saadi, while at the very bottom, in the vaults, the toughs and blades of the city hoot and bang their drums, drink arak, play dice, and dance.

Here in an evening Persians enjoy many of the things

which are important to them: poetry, water, the moon, a beautiful face. To a stranger their delight in these things may seem paradoxical, for Persians chase the golden calf as much as any people. Many of them, moreover, are beginning to complain about the scarcity of Western amusements and to ridicule the old life of the bazaar merchant, the mullah, and the peasant. Nonetheless, they take time out—much time—from the game of grab and these new Western experiments to go to the gardens and riverbanks. Above all, they will stop in the middle of anything, anywhere, to hear or quote some poetry.

Poetry in Persian life is far more than a common ground on which—in a society deeply fissured by antagonisms—all may stand. It contains, in fact, their whole outlook on life. And it is expressed, at least to their taste, in a perfect form. Poetry for a Persian is nothing less than truth and beauty. In most Western cultures today these twins have been sent away to the libraries and museums. In Persia, where practically speaking there are no museums or libraries or, for that matter, hardly any books, the twins run free.

It is perhaps difficult to conceive, but imagine that tonight on London bridge the Teddy boys of the East End will gather to sing Marlowe, Herrick, Shakespeare, and perhaps some lyrics of their own. That, at any rate, is what happens at the Khaju bridge. Boys and men go along the riverbank or to the alcoves in the top arcade. Here in these little rooms—or stages arched open to the sky and river—they choose a few lines out of the hundreds they may know and sing them according to one of the modes into which Persian music is divided. Each mode is believed to have a specific attribute—one inducing pleasure, another generosity, another love, and so on, to include all of the emotions. The singer simply matches the poem to a mode; for example, the mode of bravery to this anonymous folk poem:

They brought me news that Spring is in the plains
And Ahmad's blood the crimson tulip stains;
Go, tell his aged mother that her son
Fought with a thousand foes, and he was one. *

Or the mode of love to this fragment by a recent poet:

Know ye, fair folk who dwell on earth
Or shall hereafter come to birth,
That here, with dust upon his eyes,
Iraj, the sweet-tongued singer, lies.
In this true lover's tomb interred
A world of love lies sepulchred. . . .†

These songs (practically all Persian music, for that matter) are limited to a range of two octaves. Yet within this limitation there is an astonishing variety: design as intricate as that in the carpet or miniature, with the melodic line like the painted or woven line often flowing into an arabesque. Another striking ornament is the *chah chah,* a series of vibratos used to mark some culmination of meaning in the poem. It often rises high above the customary two octaves in a long, breaking ululation which seems to express the grief and knowledge of millennia.

It is particularly in the poems of Saadi, Hafiz, and Rumi that the *chah chah* is used most beautifully, for these are the great arias of Persian poetry. They are great partly because of their beauty and partly because they express the two deepest responses in the Persian mind—the mystic and the hedonistic. Hafiz, for example, who said that his tomb would be a place of pilgrimage for all the libertines of the world, wrote:

A flower-tinted cheek, the flowery close
Of the fair earth, these are enough for me.
Enough that in the meadow wanes and grows
The shadow of a graceful cypress-tree.
I am no lover of hypocrisy;
Of all the treasures that the earth can boast,
A brimming cup of wine I prize the most—
This is enough for me! ‡

Or Rumi, the Sufi mystic:

Lo, from the flagon of Thy love, O Lord,
My soul is swimming,
And ruined all my body's house of clay. §

Down below on the terraces the people listen: the drunks and dervishes, students, soldiers, and civil servants respond to these poems with intensity and discrimination. But they will respond even more—which shocks the stranger—if the singer is a beautiful boy.

By and large Persians are as normal in their affections as any people. But they do not restrict their love of human beauty to the opposite sex. It would seem unnatural to them, perverse; for they would argue that beauty can exist in a face as it can in a tree or a poem, quite independent of sex.

Some years ago a young and handsome khan was brought to the city to be hanged for crimes of terrorism. When the people saw him being led to the scaffold in the square, they protested until the governor agreed to spare his life. The people milling that day in the square were not a crowd of aesthetes; they were camel drivers, porters, clerks, and merchants, men who would test and judge life as they would bite a coin between their teeth. Yet to them, to kill such beauty, whatever it had done, was wrong.

This kind of attitude is half the reason for the promenade at the Khaju bridge. It is the chance to see someone—great lady, prostitute, singer, it doesn't matter whom—who has the "marks." For physical beauty, like poetry and design, must conform to a certain pattern. Skin should be the "color of wheat," the eyebrows shaped like bows, the nose long, the chin cleft, and women should be full and men straight.

*Translated by A. J. Arberry from *The Legacy of Persia* (London, Oxford University Press, 1953).
†Iraj Mirza: Translated by A. J. Arberry, *ibid.*
‡Translated by Gertrude Lowthian Bell, *Poems from the Divan of Hafiz* (London, William Heinemann, 1897).
§Translated by R. A. Nicholson from *Classical Persian Literature,* by A. J. Arberry (London, Allen & Unwin, Ltd., 1958).

EWING KRAININ

The light and shadow which envelop a seated couple and a white-garbed matron also bring out the intricate tiles that enrich the arches of the bridge.

The inevitable metaphor in Persia for a beautiful woman or man is the moon. The moon is as fixed in the Persian consciousness as it is in the sky. It appears again and again in poetry; and as we go for picnics on sunny days, so Persians go on full-moon nights. It may be the moon's coolness in a land of almost continuous sun that draws the Persians, or the way it enlivens a landscape which is often leaden. At any rate, on those nights when the moon is full, the bridge becomes a grandstand packed with people watching it.

It is a spectacle worth coming for. At the foot of those eighteen flights of steps the reflection of the bridge crosses the river in a black and terra-cotta arcade which looks almost as substantial as the bridge itself. Beyond, among the low black hills, the river spreads in pools of quicksilver, stretching on as far as the eastern mountains whose ridges glow against the sky like moonstone.

Finally, people come to the bridge because of the water there. Water is scarce in Persia. Practically all Persians, now and for generations back, have known desert thirst or seen grain wither. Also, water has strong religious associations: the weekly bath is usually a form of spiritual purification, and certain parts of the body must be washed as a preliminary to daily prayers. Water, then, means food; it means the gardens which shelter Persians from the blaze of sky and desert; and it means a kind of purity before God.

For these reasons it is usually handled as all precious things are handled, with care and with art, placed like a gem in a setting both for safety and for beauty. In the courtyards of Isfahan, water lies in a thousand pools—star-shaped pools, oval pools, long pools lined with turquoise tiles. In gardens it is led through the design like a silver thread in a tapestry. Even the big ordinary cans put outside shops in summertime, so that any passer-by may have a drink, are often topped with a trefoiled socket which holds a nosegay or a rose. And in the Chahar Bagh, the main street of the city, water flowed for centuries in marble channels.

If the water cans with their topknot of flowers are the most simple and touching tribute to water, the bridges, especially the Khaju, are often the most elaborate and impressive. A bridge is not—or at any rate never used to be—simply a means to get to the other side. It was that indeed, commodiously so, enduringly so, but it was more: for one thing, there was no hurry to get to the other side; for another, here was water.

The builders of the Khaju bridge did everything they could to delay the river, work it into patterns, and even into sounds. They designed the understructure so that it might be used, when wished, as a dam to form a lake for the royal barges or for reflecting displays of fireworks. They built cutwaters and sluices to divide the river into twenty even channels. Some of them, according to a Frenchman who was there not long after the bridge was finished, were so constructed that the water flowed through them with a "pleasing sound." On the downstream side, at either end of the bridge, they led the water into little diked-off pools; in other places they let it cascade directly from the sluices into the river; and in still other places they built terraces close to the river level over which the water fans to curl over the edge in a low white fall. Finally, they built more than sixty little rooms, forty terraces, and scores of steps, balustrades, and ledges from which to view the river.

These, then, are the things which the people come to the bridge to see. There are, of course, more ordinary things as well. There is food: corn roasted over charcoal and dipped in jars of salted water; chunks of skewer-roasted lamb wrapped in flat bread with basil, mint, and leeks; big brass pans of seeds and nuts; ice cream from carts that look like painted puppets. There are the musicians up from the teahouses of the city, their eyes bloodshot with drink and a lifetime of late nights, their hands trembling a little on the wires of their double-bellied lutes. There are the clowns, walking about with little monkeys on a leash, who are capable of saucing with bite and humor any subject in the world. There are the storytellers in brocade jester hats who chant, to the beat of a tambourine, some old tale of love or courage. There are the dancers in the vaults—dark, mustachioed lads, with a knife about them somewhere, who turn and twist in the middle of a circle of hands clapping out the rhythm. There are flowers to buy and wear behind the ear or snapped between the teeth. And there are the red and blue and yellow stars of roman candles falling like meteors around the bridge.

About ten o'clock people begin to leave the bridge. A few singers may be left in the arcade. In the vaults, certainly, a good many of the toughs will stay on, roaring toasts and insults at each other. The terraces, dark now, will still be spotted here and there with the red glow of charcoal braziers, and at the bottoms of the steps a few fishermen standing in water to their thighs may continue to work their nets. But most people will have had their evening—their time by the water, their look at the moon. Walking back through the quiet lanes, some lines of poetry they heard may run in their heads. Asleep at last in their long, empty, French-windowed rooms, they may see in their dreams a face from the bridge.

For three hundred years people have been going to the Khaju bridge. The things for which its arcades, terraces, vaults, and steps were built are still valued, and the bridge itself, strong and beautiful, still stands. Much in Persia does not—buildings, whole cities, empires have disappeared. Honesty and trust, in some places, are largely in ruins. But there is one thing in the Persian character which seems indestructible—something which continues to uphold beauty as that belt of rock in the river bed continues to support the bridge.

Terence O'Donnell is a Fulbright lecturer in English and American literature at the University of Isfahan. His first-hand acquaintance with the people of Isfahan began in 1957 while he was acting director of the Iran-America Society.

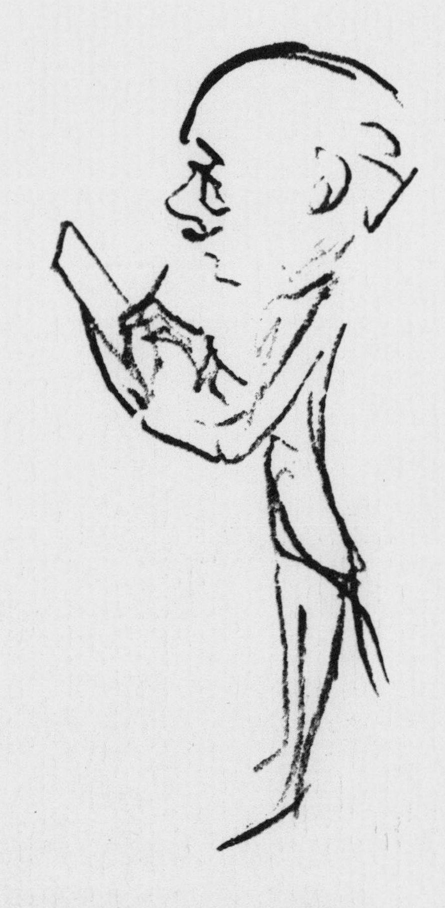

THE MAN WHO NEVER STOPPED PLAYING

By DAVID CECIL

Last December, some four years after his death, the library of Sir Max Beerbohm—the English caricaturist, essayist, novelist, and wit—was sold at the famed London auction house of Sotheby & Co. for £26,754 (roughly $75,000). This was not a collection of rare first editions to tempt the bibliomane. It was, in fact, an assortment of quite ordinary books made valuable only because Max himself had "improved" his copies of them—and the sizable sum it realized is a tribute both to his enduring reputation and to his handiwork. Some of the latter is shown in these pages. It consisted of writing fake inscriptions in the flyleaves, ingeniously altering portraits, decorating the title pages, pasting in ludicrous illustrations, and filling the margins with mischievous comments, parodies, and drawings (he often caricatured himself: the drawing above is Beerbohm as seen by Beerbohm). In short, Max was animated by the same impulse that causes the less-gifted to draw mustaches on posters, but in him it was raised to the level of art. It was not his only or greatest talent, but as the years went by it came perilously close to being the only one he chose to exercise. Some of the reasons are set forth in this article by Lord David Cecil, who is now working on a biography of Max.

Max Beerbohm's life was uneventful. It was also odd. He was born in 1872, the youngest son of a prosperous London merchant, and early showed signs of an extreme precocity. By the age of nineteen, when he was still an undergraduate at Merton College, Oxford, he was already an accomplished writer and caricaturist. What was more remarkable, he had created for himself and for the world of Oxford a finished and original personality, part *enfant terrible,* part languid, impudent, witty dandy, and with a sharp, detached, mature insight into the follies of his fellow men. Oscar Wilde met him about this time. "The gods have endowed Max," said he, "with a gift of eternal old age." Under the auspices of Wilde and others, Max presented his personality on the larger stage of London with instant success; from 1894 onward he settled down there, living in his mother's house. He had not much money, and he did not like the effort needed to make more; but he had a contented nature and modest desires, so that this did not bother him. He led a leisurely life, and his only regular occupation was to be a weekly dramatic criticism. Otherwise, every few years he produced a brief exquisite book of essays or a volume of caricatures. He was also a great social success both in the world of art and in that of fashion, and for the next fifteen years or so he was one of the most brilliant figures in London society. "How many people are there in London?" he asked a friend in later years. "Six million," was the reply. "I knew them all," said Max.

This 1891 photograph of George Bernard Shaw in his Fabian propagandist days appeared in Archibald Henderson's biography of him over the caption "The Socialist." How it looked after Max's "improvements" is shown opposite.

Suddenly, in 1910, his life changed utterly. He had always delighted in women's society, and ever since he grew up he had been involved in some kind of amorous entanglement, notably with Constance Collier, a famous beauty and actress of the Edwardian period, But his amours seem, most of them, to have been cool, elegant affairs which were not permitted to ruffle the smooth surface of his life. Now he fell seriously in love and married Florence Kahn, another actress, who came from Memphis, Tennessee. Partly because it was cheaper to live abroad, partly because he was bored with London life, he threw up his job in England and went to live in a little house near Rapallo in Italy, where, except for the periods of the two wars and for an occasional visit to arrange an exhibition of his drawings, he remained till he died in 1956. He was never to do any more regular work nor have any regular social life. From time to time friends visited him, or settled nearby. But on the whole the Beerbohms' life in Italy was preternaturally quiet. After a year or two Max hardly ever went as far as Rapallo, two or three miles away, but spent his time on the small terrace above his house or in the even smaller study, a square blue cabinlike apartment which opened onto the terrace. It might have been expected that he would give up his time to his art. Far from it. He continued to do caricatures, but not so often as in London. He hardly ever wrote at all. The literary works of his later life were nearly all composed during the few years that he was forced by political events to spend in England. How then did he occupy himself? The illustrations to this article provide the answer.

Wilde had said truly that the youthful Max was strangely mature. But the reverse was to prove equally true. The mature Max proved strangely childlike. Children—unlike grown-up people—are able to occupy themselves by "playing." "Go away and play," says the grownup to the child; and the child, if he has any imagination, can thus occupy himself indefinitely. For most people the capacity to do this goes as early as the age of nine; Max kept it till he died at eighty-four. He did not need regular work or varied companionship to be happy; he did not need to feel he was fulfilling a duty or making an impression. He wanted someone to look after the practical things of life for him and, since he was affectionate, he wanted that person to be someone he could love. His wife filled the role required. With her to act as nurse and mother he was free to retire, childlike, to an imaginary world in which he could play indefinitely.

It was a comic world: his games there were humorous games. Max was primarily a humorist, one of those rare human beings to whom the comedy of life is its most significant feature. His favorite and most natural activity was making jokes.

His study in Italy was evidence of this. On the blue walls hung a line of pictures, mostly caricatures by himself or by others like Pelligrini and Spy. Below this a single shelf of books ran round the wall. One or two of the titles made the visitor start back in surprise. What was this slender volume entitled *The Complete Works of Arnold Bennett*?

Closer inspection revealed it to be a wooden dummy elaborately disguised by Max. The title was ironical, for Bennett's greatest fault was to have written far too much. However, most of the books on the shelf were genuine. This did not protect them from Max's impish humor. Almost every one of them was scrawled over inside with pictures and comments, nine-tenths of which were humorous.

Humorous in different ways! Many kinds of jokes appealed to Max. Simple ones did. Here once more we strike the childlike strain in him: though

Beerbohm's alterations gave Shaw an ascot, a wolfish expression, and a green billycock hat. A marginal note, attributed to Henderson but actually written by Max, says the hat had belonged to Karl Marx "in his bourgeois days."

Left: Beerbohm created this most unlikely "portrait" of the urbane Henry James by pasting a woodcut of a typical Yankee on the title page of one of his books. Below: A mock presentation inscription, accurately imitating Queen Victoria's handwriting and cosy style, was written by Max in the flyleaf of her More Leaves from the Journal of a Life in the Highlands. *Opposite, top: A portrait of Rudyard Kipling, one of the few people Beerbohm did not like, was transformed into this ruthless caricature and the title altered to read "Rudyard Kipling's Soul." Opposite, bottom: Another of Max's fake inscriptions enlivens Ibsen's* When We Dead Awaken.

PARTIAL PORTRAITS

HENRY JAMES

London
MACMILLAN AND CO
AND NEW YORK
1894

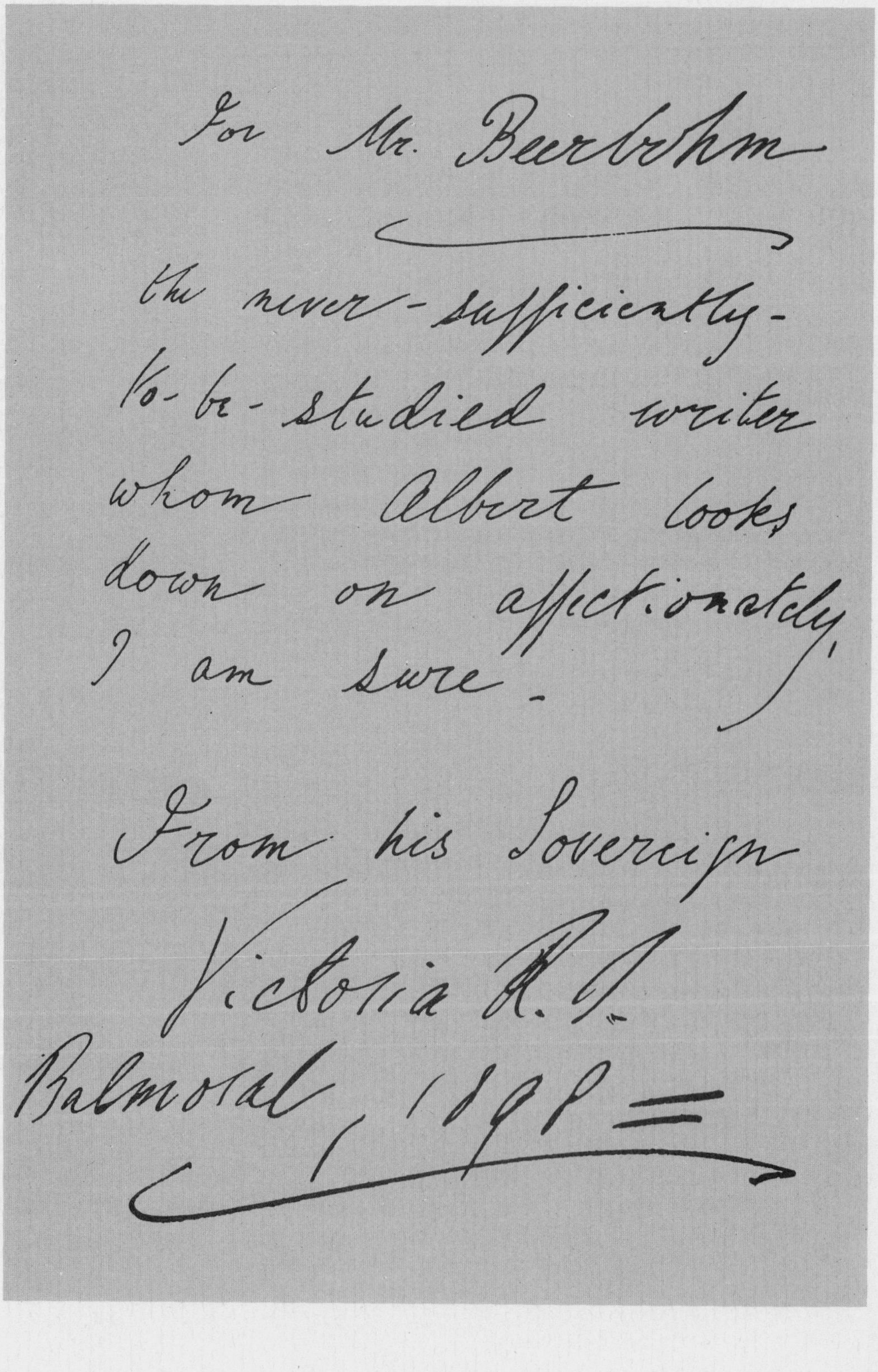

All rights reserved

For Mr. Beerbohm

the never-sufficiently-to-be-studied writer whom Albert looks down on affectionately, I am sure.

From his Sovereign

Victoria R.I.

Balmoral, 1899

For Max Beerbohm
critic of who
the writings fills
with pleasures me.
H. Ibsen
Christiania 1901.

so civilized a type, all his life he delighted in practical jokes. Even when he was over fifty he was not above making an apple-pie bed for his wife's young niece. Usually, however, Max's practical jokes were designed to disconcert the mind, not the body. Once he altered the labels in a lady's rose garden, so that when she took some guests out to see the roses, she was bewildered to find them all named after famous criminals: Betty Uprichard had become Dr. Crippen, etc.

Again, he knew a poet, Herbert Trench, who took his own work very solemnly. One of his poems was a romantic dialogue between the god Apollo and some ancient classical mariner. Max got hold of a copy of it and, with a penknife, very carefully scraped out the aspirates in all the words said by the mariner that began with *h*, substituting an apostrophe. Here is an example:

Apollo: *In what green forest inlet lay*
Her cradle and her keel?
Seaman: *I think some arm of the sea-gods*
Framed us 'er stormy frame,
And ribbed and beamed and staunchioned 'er,
And gave 'er strength a name.
Never, Sir Traveller, 'ave you seen
A sight the 'alf as fine
As when she 'ove up from the East
On our 'orizon-line!

He then sent the book to Trench, saying that he had not seen the edition before. Max had done the work so beautifully that it looked absolutely genuine. The solemn Trench was horrified and, when he discovered the truth, a little offended—till Max explained to him that he thought him a true poet, "Otherwise there wouldn't be any fun in making fun of him." However, he kept the book on his study shelf.

George Bernard Shaw was the object of his most elaborate essay in this kind of humor. Max discovered a volume of photographs of Shaw in youth. Once again, with extreme care he altered each for the worse; in one amplifying the nose, in another diverting the eyes into a squint. He then had these new versions rephotographed and sent them to various friends in England accompanied by a request to post them back to Shaw along with a letter from some imaginary fan stating that he had found the enclosed photograph of Mr. Shaw and would so much like him to sign and return it.

But of course this rollicking strain is only one element in Max's humor and not the most important. Less so, by far, than the satirical element. Untiringly Max noted the follies of mankind; and though he was too much amused by them to want them reformed, he delighted to expose them. Most of his caricatures are satirical. So also are the parodies. These are a kind of literary satire: laughing, acute criticisms of the idiosyncrasies of Henry James or Joseph Conrad or whoever happens to be his subject. His most memorable stories, too, are largely satirical. In *Zuleika Dobson* he satirizes Oxford; in *Enoch Soames* he satirizes the poets of the nineties; in *Maltby and Braxton,* fashionable life in the Edwardian era.

These stories are not only satiric. Even more are they expressions of a fantastical humor that seizes on some preposterous hypothesis and then works it out in exact and whimsical detail. The results are highly imaginative—as it were, the poetry of laughter.

All these different kinds of fun are to be found in the books in Max's study. Some are extensions or illustrations to his own writings. His copy of *The Happy Hypocrite* is ornamented with a fine flaunting sketch of Lord George Hell; that of *Zuleika Dobson* is enriched by a letter supposedly written by the heroine to George Gershwin, who many years later proposed to make an opera out of Max's story about her. I quote from it:

November 1931

Dear Mr. George Gershwin,

About a year ago, my old friend Mr. Beerbohm (if friend he can be called—for I greatly disliked his book about me; it was full of inaccuracies; and besides, why did the silly man hit on three of the least interesting and exciting days in my whole brilliant life?) told me, in great excitement, that your and his friend Mr. Charles Evans had told him that you wished to write an opera about me. I too was much excited and pleased that a musician so gifted and so eminent as you should have this idea. I don't know anything about music really, but I know what I like. Mr. Beerbohm is in rather the same rank of critic as I am. . . .

Yours sincerely,
Zuleika Kitchener

P.S. I was married, secretly, to the late Lord Kitchener, early in 1915. Being so worried by his great responsibilities at that time, he no longer had the grit to cope with my importunities, poor fellow.

Max the satirist showed himself mainly in caricature. Volumes by Shaw, William Rothenstein, and Kipling all have a caricature of the author inserted as a frontispiece. He adds some words to one of Kipling. They are not kind words. Kipling's writings represented to Max that brutal and violent side of Edwardian England which he most detested. On a title page he writes beneath Kipling's name:

the
Apocalypic [sic] *Bounder*
who
can do such fine things
but
mostly prefers to stand
(on tip-toe and stridently)
for all that is
cheap
and nasty

Max, however, is very rarely in this mood. It is not a playful mood, and he was at play in his study. Most of his alterations were done in a spirit of pure fun, farcical or fantastic. At the end of a volume of Pater's exquisite and precious studies in aestheticism, Max has appended some unexpected quotations from imagined reviews:

Some Opinions of the Press

"Preaches the doctrine of work with less perhaps than Carlyle's persuasiveness but with possibly more than Carlyle's rude vigour. . . . We have to thank him for that which his Master lacked: a robust faith in the Industrial System."

—Daily Telegraph

"Something of raucousness but much of virility. . . . Mr. Pater does not mince his words."

—Spectator

"Thor's hammer on Vulcan's anvil."

—Manchester Guardian

"At once a scourge and a purge."

—Wigan Remembrancer

On the title page he has pasted a print of a burly carpenter looking down a plank that is held in a vise and has written in pencil: "with a portrait of the Author in the act of revising his proofs."

He often inserts inappropriate portraits in this way. Conrad is represented by a spruce elderly yachtsman, Meredith by a plump plebeian countenance winking under a bowler hat. Sometimes Max alters an existing portrait. He turns Tolstoy into a Tartar-looking personage with eyeglass, plumed cap, and a gay, arch leer in his eye; Yeats is transformed into a smiling Victorian paterfamilias with spectacles and sidewhiskers. Max's masterpieces in this vein are more elaborate. There is an early example of this, a copy of Oscar Wilde's *Intentions* adorned in a mock aesthetic style with ingenious decorations. In one drawing Wilde flies through the air while an outraged John Bull tries in vain to shoot him with a bow and arrow (page 39). Even more memorable are Archibald Henderson's biography of Shaw and Queen Victoria's *More*

INTENTIONS BY
OSCAR WILDE
THE DECAY OF LYING
PEN PENCIL AND POISON
THE CRITIC AS ARTIST
THE TRVTH OF MASKS

All Rights reserved

LONDON
MDCCCXCI

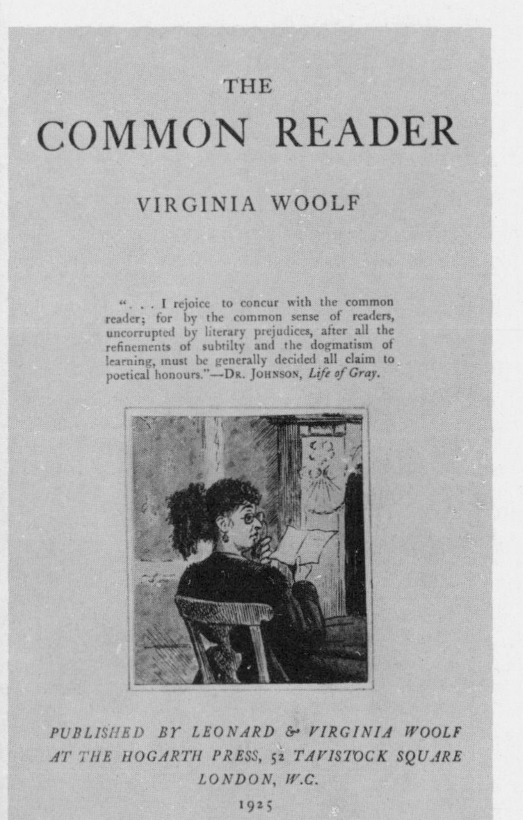

THE
COMMON READER

VIRGINIA WOOLF

". . . I rejoice to concur with the common reader; for by the common sense of readers, uncorrupted by literary prejudices, after all the refinements of subtilty and the dogmatism of learning, must be generally decided all claim to poetical honours."—DR. JOHNSON, *Life of Gray.*

PUBLISHED BY LEONARD & VIRGINIA WOOLF AT THE HOGARTH PRESS, 52 TAVISTOCK SQUARE LONDON, W.C.
1925

THE CRUISE
OF THE "NONA"
By H. BELLOC

LONDON
CONSTABLE & COMPANY LTD
1925

Some of Beerbohm's most elaborate "improvements" were made on his copy of Oscar Wilde's Intentions, *which he lavishly decorated in the style of Aubrey Beardsley. One of the drawings (upper left) shows Wilde flying through the air with a model of the Parthenon in his hands as John Bull tries to shoot him down with bow and arrow. The two title pages at the left were "improved" by pasting in Victorian woodcuts of a dowdy woman with a book—illustrating Max's, though perhaps not Virginia Woolf's, idea of the "common reader"—and a seasick couple.*

Leaves from the Journal of a Life in the Highlands. Henderson's work was the tribute of an enthusiastic hero-worshiper. It seemed so no longer when Max had put his hand to it, altering each illustration so that Shaw appeared vulgar or dissipated or absurd. Accompanying comments mock either Shaw or Henderson or the author of the illustrations; for example, on that of Rodin's bust of Shaw he writes: "The bust as conceived by Rodin was to be just a great noble mass of rough bronze with just the tip of one eyebrow protruding somewhere near the summit and several impressions of Rodin's thumb." Queen Victoria's book is an even more delightful production. Not only has Max delicately and entertainingly altered the illustrations, but he has added a number of comments in the Queen's style and also in an admirable imitation of her handwriting. I quote the line beneath a picture of the Queen's dog, Sharp: "Such a dear, faithful, noble *friend* and companion, and for whom Albert had the *greatest* respect also. Victoria R." At the beginning of the book is a dedication (reproduced here on page 36):

For Mr. Beerbohm

the never-sufficiently-
to-be-studied writer,
whom Albert looks
down on affectionately,
I am sure –

From his Sovereign

Victoria R.I.
Balmoral, 1898

Queen Victoria was a perfect subject for Max's mischievous fancy to play on. First, because she was in some ways so very comical and, second, because he liked her. Sir Theodore Martin, in his biography of Prince Albert, speaks of the Queen as "the great and good," to which Max adds "or at any rate . . . The Good and Human, the Likeable, the even Lovable; and the Peculiar, the never Uninteresting." Max is at his best when he is making fun of something he likes. He says somewhere: "Reverence is a good thing, and part of its value is that the more we revere a man the more we are struck by anything in him (and there is always much) that is incongruous with his greatness." Further, as I have said, his humor is an expression of his wish to play. A man plays most successfully when he is in a good temper.

Not that Max's interpolations are uniformly playful. Now and again we come upon a critical comment, generally expressed with a turn of wit, but in substance straightforwardly serious. In Rothenstein's *Twenty-four Portraits,* Max has written his frank and private opinion of some of his distinguished contemporaries. Robert Bridges's reputation, he says, "shows that the dismallest and driest of creative pedants may by some dispensation of kindly Fate be set high among poets." Elsewhere he is severe on the more serious type of female author. Alice Meynell wrote an essay called *Decivilised.* Under the title Max has written, "If only she could have been—just a little!"

One of his most revealing comments is on himself. Some critic had called him "the wittiest mind of an age." "No! I'm not nearly so witty as Chesterton, for one," writes Max in the margin. "But then, certainly, I haven't prostituted and cheapened my wit, as he has. How about Lytton Strachey? *There's* 'the wittiest mind of an age!'—and the virtue of it guarded still more strictly and Puritannically [*sic*] than I have guarded the virtue of mine! And I was forgetting G.B.S.!! He has prostituted his wit, certainly; and made a drudge of her too. But she can stand it. She's gigantic!" This is wonderfully detached. Max seems to have been himself one of the few writers who could set a just value on himself, neither too much nor too little. Surprisingly, this faculty was bound up with his playfulness. Since he took neither himself nor others very seriously, he was able to judge both with calm impartiality.

Max, then, was not unoccupied during the long years spent on his terrace. The odd thing was that he was satisfied by his occupation, that he could lavish so much art and care and wit and fancy on private jokes and casual comments. Most of them, moreover, were to be seen only by himself. For his wife, in spite of trying, seldom saw his jokes; and only now and again did he get to show them to a visitor. The audience he played to was himself.

Once more we must look for reasons in the childish strain in his curiously compounded nature. Along with the child's capacity for pure play, Max kept the child's ability to be completely satisfied by playing. Children are not stopped from building a sand castle by the sense that they should be doing something more important or something that would make other people admire them more. Nor was Max stopped from doodling on a title page by the desire for fame and glory or by the sense that he should be doing some serious writing. Again, children do not need an audience. They go on building the sand castle even if they know no one else will see it. So also, Max. To the end of his days his inner life retained the happy self-sufficiency of childhood.

MONUMENTS FOR OUR TIMES

Their makers face a challenge:
since old forms do not reflect life today,
to create new ones that will

Almost a century ago Walt Whitman remarked, "the day for conventional monuments, statues, memorials, &c., has pass'd away . . . they are both superfluous and vulgar." In this opinion he was several generations ahead of most of his countrymen. Until a relatively few years ago American memorial art did in fact remain conventional. Throughout our national history, until long after Whitman's day, we relied upon familiar canons that grew, with minor modifications, out of long-observed traditions. As the monuments in our civic centers, and most notably those in the city of Washington, attest, we turned almost reflexively to classical symbols and formulas to memorialize our heroes and our past—symbols and formulas that were also applied to banks and other public structures to suggest permanence and continuity.

In late years, however, these devices have been largely abandoned, as the recent competition for a memorial to Franklin D. Roosevelt so clearly demonstrated. At the beginning a group of architects and city planners advised the Congressional committee responsible for the project, "it would be well to cast aside . . . any previous building or work of art as a model to be directly imitated." In the end, of the 574 designs submitted, by far the most numerous were in a strictly modern idiom, and the jury—well balanced and highly qualified—favored only those that were.

The competition posed what has been described, aptly enough, as "an awesome artistic and social problem." It would in fact be hard to find a more demanding assignment for the contemporary artist. We may pass over the requirement, awkward though it is, that the proposed monument must take its place near the three others to Washington, Jefferson, and Lincoln without jarring these august neighbors, now so firmly established in the public regard. Such limitations, as Frank Lloyd Wright once said, can be the artist's best friends. That the monument should fittingly commemorate a man whose place in history cannot yet be defined with the same finality we accord these others presents a separate difficulty.

The very nature of the project, however, demands that it speak for our time in terms that will remain meaningful and convincing for generations still to come. Obviously, all art speaks for its time. But, just as obviously, the temper of the postwar world does not encourage the artist to think very far beyond his immediate audience.

It is a paradox that amid the plenty of American life the character of the structures we live and work in is so largely determined by factors of economy and utility—what so often amounts to little more than the cheapness and starkness of "contractor's modern." We have almost reached the point Hawthorne envisioned in his *House of the Seven Gables,* where, to escape the dead hand of the past, each generation would build for itself its own homes, its own offices, its own public structures.

There is affirmation in all this. To discard the past has become in itself an act of faith in an illimitable tomorrow. But amid the kaleidoscopic transformations of contemporary civilization we still need our permanent monuments more than ever. Visual references to our common experience, they may also be our most lasting claim on man's remembrance.

But the maker of new monuments is faced with a difficult problem of form and content: Just how is he to refer to our common experience today? What symbols is he to employ? One may agree or not with Lewis Mumford when he remarks, "Now we live in an age which has not merely abandoned a great many historic symbols, but has likewise made an effort to deflate the symbol itself by denying the values which it represents." Yet we have unquestionably abandoned the time-worn forms of memorial expression: a sculptured senatorial toga would not quite suit the late Robert A. Taft, nor would a shrine in a temple the second Roosevelt. We can no longer suggest the importance of a great man of our time by placing his effigy on horseback or at the top of a column; we must refer to the ideas and ideals he stood for. This leads inevitably to one of two results: either abstraction (the idealized allegorical figures of Justice, Virtue, Progress, and the rest, so dear to past generations, have also lost their persuasion) or the building of useful and preferably humanitarian structures dedicated to the pursuit of those ideals.

Even in what we used to think of as the timeless Orient, ancient monumental traditions have been modified in the effort to suit more effectively the climate of a modern world. The recent memorials by Yoshiro Taniguchi in Japan (page 48) have resorted to the simplest of forms—the open book, the folding screen, the commemorative inscribed stone block —to convey a quiet grace and contemporary subtlety rarely achieved in Western memorial art.

Whitman was also right in a broader sense. Where deeds of heroism or acts of tragedy have bloodied the soil, any monument runs the risk of seeming, if not vulgar and superfluous, at least ostentatious. It is the sense of place that moves us most deeply at such sites, as Lincoln forever reminded us in his Gettysburg Address. And it is this sense of place that has been respectfully observed by the unpretentious, roughhewn marker raised to the British and Canadian paratroopers who in 1944 gave their lives near Arnhem in Holland (page 44). The simple abstract form erected on the airfield at Berlin to commemorate the historic, relieving airlift there in 1948–49 (page 45) conveys a more eloquent message in our time than Generalissimo Francisco Franco's grandiose monument in The Valley of the Fallen (page 47).

The winning design for the Franklin D. Roosevelt Memorial has been criticized from many points of view, and this is hardly remarkable: the millennium will have arrived when the results of any such competition meet with ready general approval. But it is important to note that so many who are sensitive to the needs and purposes of art agree that there are more appropriate ways of saying today what was for so long confidently entrusted to the obelisk, the temple, and similar tired conventions. —MARSHALL B. DAVIDSON

SIX MEMORIALS FOR F.D.R.

The winning design in the recent Franklin D. Roosevelt Memorial Competition was the cluster of towering slabs at right. The other finalists were: Myller's chaste skylighted pavilion; Katselas's geometric canopy of reinforced concrete over a monumental bust; the Sasaki-Walker-Luders "earth sculpture"—a fountain set in a grassy hollow; a labyrinthine park by Wehrer and Borkin with a sunken plaza for award presentations; and Geller's sunburstlike composition of four ceremonial courts.

Architects: William F. Pedersen, Bradford S. Tilney and associates

Architect: Rolf Myller

Architect: Tasso Katselas

Architects: Sasaki-Walker-Luders Associates

Architects: Joseph J. Wehrer; Harold J. Borkin, associate

Architects: Abraham Geller and associates

17
SEPTEMBER
1944

Opposite: This marker in Arnhem, Holland, recalls the ill-fated attempt by British and Canadian paratroops to capture the bridges over the Rhine, and the retaliatory German bombing that destroyed part of the city. By carving the date on a broken column from the House of Justice, the sculptor created a monument of effortless strength and poignancy.

I.P.O., ROTTERDAM

ROY BERNARD CO., INC.

ROY BERNARD CO., INC.

Above: The soaring arc of the Berlin Airlift Memorial carries the eye, appropriately, up to the skies, while the ribs symbolize the three air corridors by which planes entered the city. Upper right: On Rotterdam's rebuilt waterfront a defiant bronze figure by Ossip Zadkine commemorates the city's heroism and anguish under the German bombardments of 1940. Right: What to do with the Kaiser Wilhelm Memorial Church, built in 1897, has been a subject of debate in Berlin ever since 1945. A hideous church but a magnificent ruin, it serves as a powerful reminder of the evils of war—and many wanted to keep it that way. But now Berliners are building an entirely new church behind the bomb-shattered tower.

MICHAEL BOYS

KEYSTONE PRESS

Above: A 1957 competition to design a mausoleum for Mohammed Ali Jinnah, the founder of Pakistan, was won by the London firm of Raglan Squire & Partners with the six-pointed canopy at top. Jinnah's family rejected it, however, and what will actually be built is the far more traditional mosque just above. Right: In Russia, where monumentality is no idle word, this colossal statue was one of the designs entered in a recent competition for another memorial to Lenin.

MARC RIBOUD—MAGNUM

Above: The Valley of the Fallen near Madrid is Generalissimo Francisco Franco's stupendous monument to the Civil War dead and, no doubt, to Generalissimo Franco. In addition to what meets the eye, there is a vast subterranean cathedral longer than St. Peter's. Left: The Western Hemisphere's most grandiose monument will be the Columbus Memorial Lighthouse, now under way in the Dominican Republic—a gigantic cross-shaped structure with Aztec and Egyptian overtones.

Left: Despite its initially disconcerting resemblance to a "jungle gym," this cage of white-painted tubular steel set on a cruciform base makes an appropriate and even moving memorial to the Italians who died in German prison camps during the war. It stands in a Milan cemetery and was designed by the leading Italian architectural firm of L. B. Belgioioso, E. Peressutti, and Ernesto Rogers.

CHUJI HIRAYAMA

Above: Two folding screens and a vase translated into stone by Yoshiro Taniguchi make an effective memorial to the Japanese doctor-poet Mokutaro Kinoshita. Opposite: One of America's most arresting monuments—a fluted dome by Philip Johnson over a Jacques Lipchitz sculpture—commemorates nineteenth-century utopian communities in Indiana.

A FLOURISH

Trust the theater not to leave a rich vein unmined for long. Since audiences first found pleasure in watching performers mime the frailties of man, entrepreneurs have struck gold-bearing ore in a seam of material as old as society: the way of the harlot. And because the theater has ever sought the suspension of belief in crass reality, its ladies of easy virtue usually have been furnished with hearts of gold—the oldest profession has provided the theater with its oldest cliché, and the refinements wrung from it have exercised masters of the drama from Menander to Tennessee Williams. So much comfort do men seem to find in this myth that playwrights have obliged by making some of their most memorable women fallen ones, and audiences have taken to their hearts such trollops as Marguerite Gautier, Sadie Thompson, Anna Christie, and Blanche DuBois. But even beside this historic if tarnished roster, the plethora of *poules* which has been visited on the New York theater during the current season—both off Broadway and on—deserves remark.

Accordingly, HORIZON presents a gallery of talented ladies of the theater who have been impersonating, if not outright doxies, at least wanton creatures, no better than they might be. At left, prancing on to introduce her colleagues as it were, is the lissome Arnette Jens of

OF STRUMPETS

The Balcony, Jean Genet's fantastical play at off-Broadway's Circle in the Square. It is the conceit of M. Genet that the actress who portrays a certain occupant of a French bagnio should be attired as a horse to please her client, who dreams of himself as a general. Next in this tableau is Elizabeth Seal, the wistful heroine of *Irma la Douce.* Miss Seal has captured the heart of Broadway as Irma, the enchanting gamin of the streets of Montmartre, who remains unsullied in spirit because she takes money only from the man she loves. The quizzical individual at center is Avis Bunnage, who here comports herself as the archpriestess of the bizarre Dublin kip in which Brendan Behan has set *The Hostage.* This admirable actress also created the role of Helen, the errant mother, in the original London production of Shelagh Delaney's *A Taste of Honey.* And it is as this same Helen in the New York production of Miss Delaney's play that Angela Lansbury—the next in the group—gives a triumphant performance, presenting a raffish charmer at once brazen and winsome. The gallery closes with the comely Eileen Rodgers. As a brass-lunged, heart-of-gold, high-priced lady, she is a principal attraction of *Tenderloin,* the musical play which commemorates New York's gaudy turn-of-the-century quarter in which characters resembling these five flourished.

Photographs by MILTON H. GREENE

THE MOVIES MAKE HAY WITH THE CLASSIC WORLD

By PETER GREEN

Unlimited splendor, slaughter, villainy, lust—these are the distinguishing characteristics of ancient Greece and (in particular) Rome, as revealed in a fast-lengthening line of Hollywood epics. How this celluloid image strikes an Englishman whose notions about antiquity stem from somewhat soberer sources is described here by Peter Green, the essayist and novelist who was formerly the director of classical studies at Selwyn College, Cambridge. His comments find an accompaniment—indeed a parallel—in the illustrations on these pages by another Englishman, John Leech, who was Punch*'s leading artist a century ago; they appeared first as etchings for* The Comic History of Rome, *a sequel by Leech and Gilbert à Beckett to their* Comic History of England *(see* HORIZON *for March, 1960).*

"History made Spartacus die in his last battle: Super Technirama-70 reserves Kirk Douglas for an unkinder fate."

The spectacular screen epic has been with us almost as long as the film industry itself. The two grew up together. Moguls such as Cecil B. de Mille and D. W. Griffith gave the genre its pristine shape, from which subsequent producers and directors have diverged at their peril. From *Intolerance* to *Spartacus*, from the first to the latest version of *Ben-Hur*, the formula has survived virtually unchanged. The plot is normally vestigial, the characterization perfunctory to a degree. Remarks which would make the most trivial pulp novelist squirm with shame here form the common currency of the script. Costume and background, on the other hand, all the outward and visible signs of antiquity, have the most scrupulous attention lavished upon them. Dramatic climaxes are supplied on a vast and impersonal scale: earthquakes or eruptions, with lavish sets collapsing like packs of cards; battles ashore or afloat, involving upward of ten thousand extras; or, to take a recent notable example, a really stunning chariot race. Cruelty is always well to the fore; the crack of the rawhide whip goes echoing down every sound track, and gallons of trickling studio blood are shot in relentless close-up. Private life in the normal sense goes almost unregarded, promiscuous sexuality in some form or other is more or less *de rigueur*, and whenever possible the mixture is laced with a shot of primitive (and vaguely sentimentalized) Christianity.

These common characteristics, taken together, suggest that what we are dealing with here is our old friend the Archetypal Myth. If this is so, the phenomenon is well worth a closer look, since far from dating back to man's preliterate childhood, it has arisen directly as a result of the Industrial Revolution. The greatest mistake anyone could make in analyzing a spectacular epic is to assume that its underlying motivation has any direct connection with the ancient world. A serious-minded director or producer who wants to crash the Greco-Roman preserve is faced by certain iron conventions of the genre. You aren't forced to like them, but you can't change them, and it would be idiotic to try.

The most psychologically suggestive point about this kind of film is that the really abysmal ones do, if anything, rather better at the box office than those —such as *Spartacus, Ben-Hur,* or *Alexander the Great*—which make strenuous efforts in the direction of historical veracity or characterization in depth. According to a survey conducted by *Films and Filming,* the most successful film shown in Britain during the year that ended October 31, 1960—not even, be it noted, the most successful *historical* film but the winner against all comers —was *Hercules Unchained,* that tottering vehicle for Steve Reeves and his muscles. If *Spartacus* and *Ben-Hur* overhaul this extraordinary film as money spinners, let not their producers flatter themselves that such an achievement is due primarily to the way they handle, say, the ethics of slavery or Christianity in Judaea. It will be because of Kirk Douglas's physique; and the gladiatorial battles; and the flogging aboard the galleys; and Stephen Boyd, flayed to a crimson pulp, gurgling up blood in his last death agony; and the splendor, the panoramic sweep, which the wide screen brings to a marching Roman army in full accoutrement. Authenticity is a top-dressing, no more, to a far more basic and crude formula.

The Industrial Revolution had many queer by-products, ranging from Luddites and antirailroad fanatics to the rural utopian dreams of William Morris and Richard Jefferies. But the predominant motif was one of escape, and it has remained with us ever since: escape from the soot-ridden, clangorous horrors of urban life, escape from a drab, regimented, commercial age, escape from repetitive jobs and gray horizons. And what avenues were opened up for such disillusioned fugitives, those who could not face the iron here-and-now? Perhaps science fiction was the most promising, and still is: it operates both in time and space. The addict can shift himself both into the future and on to another planet. But historical fiction also had its possibilities. It was in the late nineteenth century that there began to appear that spate of hardy perennials about antiquity—*Ben-Hur, Quo Vadis, The Sign of the Cross*—which set a pattern, established a myth, and have, not surprisingly, become a staple of the film industry. (One was reminded of this with a jolt when two Neros, Peter Ustinov and Charles Laughton, from *Quo Vadis* and *The Sign of the Cross* respectively, turned up together in *Spartacus.*) Hollywood did not invent the formula; it was there already. The film moguls, as usual, simplified it, stereotyped it, reduced it to the ultimate in absurdity, and made it sell. No, perhaps not even that: the psychological demand was there, vast and clamoring, and all they had to do was to feed it raw meat.

If the formula was, dramatically speaking, puerile, its sociohistorical implications were, and remain, most revealing. One great and obvious relief brought by even the worst of such films is the way in which they simplify life, slow it down to something approaching a natural rhythm. There are no machines, no modern communication systems, no car-jammed city streets, no guns, no airplanes. The fastest moving object in view is a galloping horse or a slave-driver's whip. No one in this world can annihilate space by picking up a telephone or looking into a TV screen. Mass production is virtually unknown. Every object has been produced individually, and the whole business of life is intimately bound up with human handiwork. There is a strong, if often subconscious, streak of William Morris in every city dweller; and by watching such films it gets an unsuspecting field day.

This does not explain, however, just why it is the world of antiquity that has particularly attracted our modern mythmakers' attention. Would not any society before the end of the eighteenth century meet the case just as well? What special qualities reside in the cultures of Rome, Greece, Carthage, or Egypt to make them so irresistible to film makers? First, and perhaps most important, they are distant enough from our own times to be free of any concrete historical associations. They can be mythicized without a constant intrusion of hard and awkward facts. Secondly, and hardly less relevant, their colorful costumes and artifacts offer a compensatory visual feast for men in gray flannel suits. Thirdly, they were societies which took slavery in their stride and therefore provide endless opportunities for exploiting the cult of violence with plausible historical justification. Fourthly, they had a code of sexual ethics happily unclouded by guilt morality: this, superficially considered, could be held to sanction almost any interpretative salacity. Finally, as a counterweight to the release of the pagan id, there was always the life of Christ or the suffering of the early Christians; and as both these themes could carry their own ration of violence and bloodshed as well as uplifting religious *cachet,* producers have always tended (with, no doubt, the very best of mixed motives) to bring them in wherever possible.

It is significant, too, that for every one film made about Greece there are, at a conservative estimate, at least five set in Rome; and the fact that Christ's ministry coincided chronologically with imperial Rome at its apogee cannot wholly explain this preponderance. (Latterly, Carthage has been intruding into the picture, too, and Flaubert, of all people, may have to take some of the blame here. There is enough torture, sadism, and general exotic nastiness in *Salammbô* to glut the most exacting wide-screen orgiast: a new film of the book, not surprisingly, is on the stocks.) The unpalatable truth of the matter is that Roman and Carthaginian social mores are a good deal more congenial—and indeed more familiar—to twentieth-century public taste than those we associate with the violet-crowned city of Pericles. The modern cinema-goer who sits eagerly through *Carthage in Flames*

"A marching Roman army in full accoutrement"

or *The Last Days of Pompeii* is not only retreating into a compensatory dream world but identifying that world, at one remove, with several salient features of his own. Thus what finally hits his psyche is a curdling mixture of truth and fantasy, modern fact and ancient near-fiction.

Consider the Romans as we think of them today. They were greedy, intemperate, promiscuous, authoritarian, and materialistic. Though they preserved a faint streak of peasant superstitiousness, they had largely lost the inner religious sense, and compensated for this with elaborate ritual flummery on public occasions. Their main aim in life was making and spending money, in which pursuit they were egged on by domineering wives. They were shrewd speculators and financiers, somewhat contemptuous of foreigners, yet at the same time anxious to acquire foreign culture. They paid inflationary prices for Greek works of art but produced little of real merit themselves. Their divorce rate, especially in the upper echelons, was phenomenal. They treated their slaves with quite incredible brutality, till they found that such a policy was economically unsound. They believed in using strong discipline, especially abroad and upon their crack troops. They had a natural talent for road building, lawmaking, administration, and all practical problems. Abstract thought irked them. Food and sex they enjoyed in almost exactly the same way. The Carthaginians had all the nastier Roman vices without their redeeming virtues, being morose, commercial-minded *in excelsis,* actively antipathetic to the arts, and given to roasting children alive in moments of crisis.

Any contemporary reader who examines this catalogue of characteristics will find a good number of them uncomfortably familiar to him: the Roman here portrayed might almost be a delinquent member of the Affluent Society as delineated by Professor Galbraith. And here, I am afraid, we begin to see just why films about ancient Rome are so popular. The spectator—*Homo urbanus,* if you like—is confronted with a hero whose values and outlook are akin to his own, *but whose behavior, as sanctioned by society, is wholly different.* This celluloid alter ego, with his high boots, rippling muscles, ready sword, and authoritarian habits, is a most potent violence surrogate. He can flog slaves to his heart's content, pluck women like ripe apples, intrigue, murder, wear the most gorgeous fancy dress all day long, and ride safely into the sunset at the end of the last reel. A Roman guise suits him very well.

It is not surprising, indeed, that many of these films (not always the worst, either) should have a faint but unmistakable undertone of fascism about them. Ever since they cranked out *Cabiria* in 1914, the Italians have produced more classical spectacle than most other film-making countries, and d'Annunzio and Il Duce between them made quite a few modern additions to the original rods and axes of the S.P.Q.R. The more grandiosely repulsive propaganda that crept into such films during Mussolini's regime vanished abruptly after the war, to be replaced by less politically oriented battles, orgies, and flagellations. Jackboots were out, breasts were in: 1953 saw Sophia Loren featured (complete with asp) in a production called *Due notti con Cleopatra.*

As in the cognate art of pornography, we have here a significant inversion of normal emphasis and purpose. In a pornographical novel, plot, characterization, narrative technique, and style are all subordinated to the author's main purpose—that is, of introducing sexual episodes at regular intervals (regardless of dramatic probability) with the deliberate intention of stimulating a responsive thrill in the reader. They have no other real function. Now while these Italian films are certainly not pornographic, they do display an almost identical inversion of emphasis. No enthusiast will complain about the frightful dialogue, the gross historical inaccuracies, the bad acting, or the incompetent direction; these are purely incidental to the episodic ritual thrills of flagellation, incendiarism, swordplay, cloak swirling, and innocent, if garish, public orgies. *Hercules Unchained* has been described as a "vehicle" for Mr. Reeves, and for once the description is clinically quite accurate.

This type of film, which critics regard as beneath their contempt, and which does not even rate a New York or London screening before general distribution, nevertheless embodies the *mythos* of film epic in its purest and most potent form. Any director or producer who aims to make a *serious* film about the ancient world will ignore the rule at his peril. Such a production (*Alexander the Great* was the classic instance) breaks up the ritual pattern, brings the cold wind of reality into a traditional and carefully preserved dream world. The whole essence of popular historical spectacle is that it shall bear no conceivable resemblance to real life or actual human behavior. We simply cannot visualize the private life of the characters in these films: they only exist for the moment of action; they embrace in a social void. One may as well inquire what happens to the Little Swans when that famous *pas de quatre* finally vanishes into the wings.

To treat any society in such sub-balletic terms at once imposes an almost insurmountable barrier between us and it. Furthermore, in the case of classical antiquity, this illusion is actually heightened by the kind of evidence which has survived the centuries. Stone endures, fabric does not; and thus any attempt to re-create a Greek or Roman living room has a curiously bare quality about it. There is no clutter of bric-a-brac, no evidence of *living*: the general impression is of a bleak and paradoxically modernistic hotel foyer. Similarly with the literary evidence, so selectively concerned with public affairs: it requires a strenuous effort of the imagination to picture ancient Greeks or Romans doing anything except fighting battles, making speeches, or lounging about over their wine discussing the True, the Good, and the Beautiful. It is somehow symbolic of this imaginative failure that in almost every historical spectacle I have seen, both costumes and streets have been impeccably *clean*, as though soused in detergents for the occasion.

"Rippling muscles, ready sword, and authoritarian habits"

Robert Rossen cheerfully broke this and most of the other unwritten laws when filming *Alexander*: he chose for King Philip's Macedonian capital, Pella, not the usual fantasy set (by Karnak, out of Grand Central Station) but a chaotic, tumble-down hillside village, its rutted, stony tracks thick with dust, dung, and errant hens.

Nothing could better demonstrate the power of the myth than the reception accorded to this splendid (and splendidly intelligent) production. It was, significantly, written, produced, and directed by Rossen himself. Despite Robert Krasker's brilliant use of the wide screen—his battle scenes in particular were shot with a superb mastery and sense of composition—and a star-studded cast that included Richard Burton, Fredric March, and Claire Bloom, the critics (with some honorable exceptions) were lukewarm, and the public actively bored. It is not hard to see why. The dialogue was adult, the characterization extremely subtle: the strutting Technicolor figures of myth had suddenly flung off their masks and emerged as genuine human beings. Historically, apart from an inevitable heightening of Alexander's doubtful amatory interests and a routine foreshadowing of Christianity ("If God is the Father, then *He* is the Father of all"), the production adhered to the known facts with quite astonishing fidelity. The script included quotations, verbatim, from Homer, Aristotle, and Euripides; and several of Plutarch's best anecdotes (Philip drunk after Chaeronea, for instance—a pygmy figure dancing among the dead, the mountains echoing and mocking his minuscule triumph) were used with tremendously telling effect. For me this film was a triumph, a vindication of what could be done with the past in the way of imaginative re-creation. But Mr. Rossen broke the rules and ignored the conventions. *Alexander the Great* was not what Hollywood regards as a success; there is little doubt that other producers observed the omens and took appropriate action.

The problem facing them, clearly, was this: How could a formula be evolved that somehow reconciled the idea of a "quality" production with the peculiar (but financially important) de-

"A code of sexual ethics happily unclouded by guilt morality"

mands of the myth addicts who finally footed the bill? The industry as a whole had come to see that spectacle was its best weapon against television's slow encroachment. But prestige, if nothing else, demanded something better than the kind of rubbish being churned out monthly at Cinecittà. To judge by the two most notable productions released during the last year or so—*Ben-Hur* and *Spartacus*—the answer was to make something so big, so visually impressive, so spectacular in every sense of the word, that a little subtle acting and serious intent could be slipped in without any noticeable loss at the box office. *Ben-Hur* had the further advantage of being a remake, and from a perennially popular novel into the bargain.

It is very easy to be stunned by the sheer *size* of *Ben-Hur* into taking it rather more seriously than it deserves. As pure spectacle, certainly, it is, without parallel, the most ambitious and grandiose epic ever screened. But spectacle, fundamentally, it remains, despite script-writers' credits to Christopher Fry, S. N. Behrman, Gore Vidal, and Maxwell Anderson, some dickering with Jewish nationalism, and a rather more than usually realistic piece of make-up work in the matter of leprosy. None of the old familiar ingredients had been altered; they were merely blown up to gigantic proportions. The usual fuss was made about authentic sets and costumes (the former including a seventy-five-foot-high replica of the Joppa Gate), and the film abounds in whips, blood, burning ships, brawny booted legionaries, and all the rest of the essential symbolic panoply. Slaves toil sickeningly at their oars, under the hot sardonic eye of Jack Hawkins, who (as the fictional Admiral Quintus Arrius) has clearly done plenty of anachronistic homework on the nicer points of sadomasochism. The Calvary motif, though more reticently handled than usual, remains, obstinately, a gimmick: genuine religious feeling seems to come hard to Hollywood directors, who make do instead with glucose sentimentality, bloodstained suffering, and melodramatically improbable miracles. Above all, there is that breathtaking (and, let it be said, exceedingly unpleasant) chariot race. When you get down to brass tacks, it has no more organic connection with the plot than a special turn in a musical; but it does offer unique opportunities for sensationalism—a colossal set, thousands of extras, thundering hoofs, and above all, the spectacle of a man flayed alive into a raw, bleeding pulp, relentlessly scrutinized in close-up.

It is a pity that preoccupation with "realism" of this sort could not occasionally be diverted into more useful channels. But the old leopard of spectacle is loath to change his spots, and strange anomalies still creep into even the most glossily expensive production. Take the incident of Ben-Hur's house, for instance. This is a large and luxurious mansion, situated in the best residential quarter of Jerusalem, where the ground rent alone must have cost heaven knows how many shekels (or sesterces) a square yard. Yet during its owner's enforced absence as a galley slave, this valuable property remains so utterly uninvestigated that Esther and her old crippled father can lurk there, undetected, for at least five years, while the place slowly decays around them. No requisitioning, no forced sale, not even a tax inspection. Ben-Hur's home is a kind of impregnable enclave, unrelated to Jerusalem at all in the script writer's imagination.

There is another, and somewhat more alarming, feature which *Ben-Hur* and the more recent *Spartacus* have in common. Both films are explicitly concerned with liberal, not to say revolutionary, movements against Rome. Spartacus the slave leader and Judah Ben-Hur the Jewish nationalist are brothers under the skin. We hear a good deal about freedom, justice, and the rights of man in either case. Yet while our sympathies are ostensibly engaged with the underdog, the victim of occupation or enslavement, there is at the same time a very powerful undercurrent of emotion tugging in precisely the opposite direction —toward Roman discipline, Roman law and order, Roman materialism. The film makers seem bemused despite themselves by those well-drilled legions, those curt-

"The episodic ritual thrills of flagellation, incendiarism, swordplay, cloak swirling, and garish public orgies"

ly efficient governors, the whole apparatus of benevolent or not-so-benevolent paternalism. The result is that in both films the moral emphasis gets oddly misplaced. Arrius, in the long run, is the man on whom we would rely, not Ben-Hur. Spartacus, for all his heroics, cuts a very shabby picture beside the rich, coolheaded, practical Crassus. This curious (and I am sure unintentional) phenomenon may serve to remind us that it is the authoritarian, not the rebel, whom the cult of violence best serves.

Any hopes that *Spartacus* was going to be a really serious or honest film were shattered in advance by the news that its makers had bought the wrong novel. To choose Howard Fast's doctrinaire writing over Arthur Koestler's *The Gladiators* seemed clear proof that political honesty, at least, was going by the board: and so, in the event, it turned out.

The tragedy of the gladiators' revolt lay in the central, unpalatable truth that it collapsed mainly through inner dissension, corruption of purpose, squabbling among the slave leaders, flawed idealism. Koestler saw all this, with stony clarity, and the result was one of the most memorable novels about ancient Rome written in the last fifty years. But Fast (and presumably producer-star Kirk Douglas and director Stanley Kubrick) would have none of such dangerous stuff. What they wanted was no more than a straightforward variant on the old cut-and-dried epic morality, a clash between brutal Romans and heroic slaves.

The very considerable distortion of historical truth which *Spartacus* displays aims always at underlining this simple contrast. Spartacus's more cruel exploits are discreetly whitewashed and his proconsular pretensions ignored. Crassus, on the other hand, is presented, gratuitously, both as a homosexual and a would-be dictator, for neither of which charges is there one shred of evidence. (His premature promotion from Praetor to First Consul was probably done for the benefit of those groundlings unfamiliar with the niceties of Roman rank. One great headache for every producer in this field must be getting round the annual change of office at Rome—a democratic habit which spells death to filmic continuity.) History made Spartacus die in his last battle: Super Technirama-70 reserves Kirk Douglas for an unkinder fate. He is perfunctorily crucified outside Capua (strange how gory realism balked at representing *this* horror; but then, after all, crucifixion carries no sadistic undertones and might conceivably be thought blasphemous), and looks down, Christlike, in most genteelly simulated agony, at Jean Simmons holding his newborn son. The *mythos* has triumphed again.

What, then, is the upshot of the whole matter? One thing seems clear: so long as the wide screen and expensive color processing remain prime requirements for making films about antiquity (with a half dozen or more top-notch stars thrown in to swell the budget), the genre will continue to be subservient to the old traditions and shibboleths, if only for financial reasons. *Alexander the Great* can have no successors. The only hope, it seems to me, is for a director such as Michael Cacoyannis to have a shot at the impossible—say a film of the Peloponnesian War in narrow-frame black-and-white, with no international stars and a shoestring budget. Rome must be severely left alone for a while; Greece offers far better opportunities. (It is significant that even the worst films set in Greece show some spark of imagination: look at *Ulysses* and *The Giant of Marathon.*) Meanwhile it is encouraging to note that Hollywood, too, is looking toward Greece. Shooting has just finished on *The Lion of Sparta,* which, as you might guess, is all about Thermopylae and Leonidas: there is an encouraging cast (David Farrar, Richard Egan, Sir Ralph Richardson), much of the action has been filmed *in situ,* and reports suggest that the treatment is reasonably accurate. (Why not, indeed? You couldn't get a better or more filmworthy subject if you tried.) And the indefatigable Jules Dassin is having a go at Pericles. If *he* can't knock the Olympian off his marbled and Thucydidean pedestal, who can? Perhaps history on celluloid is on the upgrade after all.

Romanticism has been called, variously, "the rebirth of wonder"; "the pursuit of beauty through rebellion"; "the cult of the extinct"; "all that is not Voltaire." Its critics disagree, even as the romantics themselves disagreed as to what they were after; but everyone would agree that Percy Bysshe Shelley, poet of exquisite sensibility, and political and social rebel besides, was an arch-romantic.

He was twenty-nine when he went down with his sailboat on a stormy day in the Gulf of Spezia in 1822. When his ashes were buried in Rome, among those at the ceremony was the English painter Joseph Severn, who twenty-three years later painted this memorial canvas, *Shelley Composing "Prometheus Unbound" in the Baths of Caracalla,* now hanging in the Roman villa preserved as a shrine to another great expatriate, John Keats, who died there.

The delicate, wraithlike Shelley of this elegiac portrait looks less like an apostle of revolt than like the "beautiful and ineffectual angel" the sturdy Victorian critic Matthew Arnold saw in him. Yet Shelley was all revolution—never more so than just when gathering inspiration amid Roman ruins for his dramatic poem on Prometheus's own revolt against the

KEATS-SHELLEY MEMORIAL HOUSE, ROME—SCALA

gods. Himself the enemy of established mores, churches, princes, and powers, Shelley saw his lyric stanzas as clarion calls for a better world of brotherhood. His passions, the convulsions of his personal life and of those closest to him, his melancholy over what was lost, and his ardent hopes for what might yet come, all placed him at the storm center of a movement of which he remains one of the supreme embodiments.

THE Romantic REVOLT

Young rebels turned against Europe's Old Order to fight its restraints and artifice in the cause of boundless self-expression and reform. Although their passions led to many an extreme, their legacies have served to enlarge the individual spirit of Western man

By HAROLD NICOLSON

ROUSSEAU

"Romanticism," wrote Taine, "imposed itself by opposing everything that had preceded it." Later critics have contested this pragmatic judgment and have contended that the divergence between classicism and romanticism is not clear-cut. They are able to show that elements of pure romanticism can be discovered even in the works of Alexander Pope, whereas Byron, who in the early nineteenth century was hailed as the mighty hierophant of the romantic movement, became wearied of his own *Childe Harold* and ended by advocating a more classic mode.

It has thus today become the fashion to disapprove of the terms "classic" and "romantic" as designating a contrast between two distinct shades of thought and feeling, and to contend that the careless use of these two labels may obscure the essential continuity of letters. I disagree with such assimilations. I am convinced that in the latter half of the eighteenth century people did in fact become tired of the old doctrines of symmetry or "correctness" and came to attach importance to freer and more individual methods of self-expression. A similar revolution in taste has occurred in our own century, when the old habit of direct communication of meaning has in art, as well as in poetry, been superseded by new methods of suggesting meaning through association of ideas. The older generation find the new allusive method incomprehensible; the younger generation regard the literary fashions of their parents as uninteresting. The continuity of letters is of course preserved to the extent that mankind will always strive to express beauty; but what to one generation appears eternal beauty will to the next appear stupid and stale. Nor should such transitions of taste and interest, even when abrupt, be dismissed as insignificant: they represent the development, and even the progress, of the aesthetic sense. It is this progress that we have inherited from the Romantic Revolt.

I quite agree with Taine that the romantics, in Germany, in England, and in France, *did* think and feel entirely differently from their classic forebears. They preferred freedom to order, adventure to conformity, surprise to recognition, imagination to correctness, the natural to the artificial, the irregular to the regular, individual experience to tradition. They argued that their aims represented a "return to nature," although they interpreted the word "nature" in many different ways. To some it meant no more than a simpler way of life, in contrast to the rush and rattle of civilized society. To others it signified "freedom"; namely, a return to a primitive age "when wild in woods the noble savage ran," before bad laws and artificial institutions had come to corrupt the virtue of the Golden Age. To others again it suggested religious liberty, a worship of the wonders of nature as contrived and regulated by a Divine Artificer who was above theological dogma and whose relation to mankind was more intimate than anything provided by the rituals of the established churches. To some it represented the peace and quiet of natural scenery, the solitude of woods and remote valleys, or the awe-inspiring majesty of mountains, waterfalls, and precipices.

BYRON

The age of sensibility abolished the frigid eighteenth-century dislike of overt emotion and the contempt of men of culture for anything savoring of what they called "ugly enthusiasm." The classic contention that it was improper for any artist to reveal himself, the old motto *le moi est haïssable,* were replaced by the new habit of offering to the public "the pageant of a bleeding heart" and of revealing not only one's personal melancholy and guilt but also one's sins and passions. Rousseau regarded his *Confessions* as a portrait of "the natural man"; Byron devoted his great gift of rhetoric to depicting in *Childe Harold* a sated hedonist who sought to discover in distant countries and uncivilized surroundings the lost stimulus of passion. The satiety of Childe Harold, as the *Weltschmerz* of Werther or the distress and disgust of Chateaubriand's René, became symptoms of what has been described as *le mal du siècle.*

It is important to remember that Byron, on attaining incomparable success, became bored by his own romanticism; that Goethe, on becoming an excellent civil servant in Weimar, repudiated poor Werther; and that Chateaubriand ended by becoming the champion of the established church and a conventional, and extremely vain, diplomatist. Thus it can be said that romanticism, which began as a heresy, had not sufficient vitality to establish itself as a doctrine. Yet from 1760 onwards it assuredly transformed the feelings and the thoughts of man.

GOETHE

Since the days of Langland and Chaucer, English literature had always contained a powerful "romantic" element; and the British genius has always tended to prefer freedom to correctness, individual experience to established doctrine, the inductive to the deductive, imagination to reason, the inconsequent to the logical, the serpentine to the rectilinear. During the first great phase of English literature, the period from Spenser to Milton, British dramatists and poets reveled in the variety of human adventure and the luxuriance of a rich language. To the French, who had already been taught by Boileau that all excess of feeling or expression was an error of taste, British authors appeared to be men of unkempt savagery, as exotic as today are the Australian aborigines. Voltaire, who lived several years among the English and who acquired some respect for their political sagacity and their reverence for law, continued to regard them as barbarians in intellectual and aesthetic realms. He considered that even Shakespeare, for all his incontestable genius, was, from the literary aspect, comparable only to a Hottentot yodeling in the swamps. And Voltaire during two-thirds of the eighteenth century was the recognized dictator of literary fashion.

The teaching of Boileau, the doctrine of "correctness," crossed the Channel early in the eighteenth century, and by 1733 Pope had established himself as the high priest of reason and good sense. The British, I am glad to say, are not by nature reasonable, and it was not long before the Augustan Age of English literature produced a reaction. British writers thereafter reverted to the more natural habits of individual expression and free association.

This article is mainly concerned with the elements of the Romantic Revolt that are operative today. It does not deal with the metaphysical and social results of the revolt, but with the cult of "sensibility" which it introduced and fostered, and with the transformation it effected in man's attitude toward "nature." If we are to understand the suddenness and completeness of that transformation, we can take as an illustration the quick change of attitude toward the art of garden design. This was not a mere by-product of the revolt. It was the earliest symptom of a reaction against the formal; the widest, most rapid, most complete, and most detailed example of the reversal of taste and awareness. Those who contend that in fact there was little difference between the classic and romantic must admit that the change from the classic to the romantic concept of garden design was abrupt, creative, and universal. It illustrates the completeness with which, within two generations, men can change their attitude toward the outside world.

COLERIDGE

Dr. Johnson was not a romantic. He had no taste for natural beauty. "A blade of grass," he remarked to Mrs. Thrale, "is always a blade of grass: men and women are *my* subjects of enquiry." Whenever Boswell displayed symptoms of becoming romantic, he was sharply snubbed by his formidable companion. Yet Boswell was a natural romantic, and we can observe in his diaries not merely all the symptoms of sensibility but even those of a Werther-like preoccupation with melancholy (which he called "hypochondria") and guilt. These guilt sensations arose from the decline in religious faith and the growth of skepticism.

The conflict of dogma and the religious wars which followed the Reformation inevitably produced a reaction against dogmatic theology and the discipline of the churches. Voltaire taught men to regard both the tyranny of the Jesuits (which he

TEXT CONTINUED ON PAGE 64

The most famous poem of England's new century inspired this painting by its most adventurous artist: J. M. W. Turner's *Childe Harold's Pilgrimage*. When the first two cantos of Byron's epic of that name appeared in 1812, the young poet overnight became the hero of a vast public that was carried away by this exuberant chronicle of his own adventures in exotic, perfumed settings. Four years later the unsavory scandal of his divorce led to his self-exile from England and his pursuit of deeper musings and riper loves in Italy. The writing of *Childe Harold* went on; and it is the maturer mood of the final, fourth canto, with its search for refuge and its nostalgic communing with the past, that Turner tried to capture in this canvas painted during his own Mediterranean sojourn after Byron's death. The landscape of the work is imaginary, and it presents no actual scene from the poem; but when it was first shown at

BY COURTESY OF THE TRUSTEES OF THE TATE GALLERY, LONDON

the Royal Academy in 1832. Turner asked that there be printed in the exhibition catalogue under its title the lines from Byron's fourth canto (stanza xxvi) beginning, ". . . and now, fair Italy, / Thou art the garden of the world, the home / Of all Art yields, and Nature can decree; / Even in thy desert, what is like to thee?"

Born many rungs below Lord Byron on the social scale, Turner had started life as a Cockney barber's son—yet had precociously exhibited at the Royal Academy at the age of fifteen, painting accomplished canvases in the approved literal style. In his mature years, though, he too responded to the new romantic impulses and took to painting highly personal impressions in which solid forms were broken up under the play of spontaneous, poetic, often nebulous light. A pioneer in his pursuit of luminous color (see also his *Rain, Steam and Speed,* page 88), he prefigured the era of Monet and Degas.

TEXT CONTINUED FROM PAGE 61

much exaggerated) and the asceticism of the Puritans and the Jansenists as "infamous superstitions." During the Age of Reason most men of culture proclaimed themselves to be deists who regarded Jehovah as an absurd Hebrew legend and sought their deity in a Divine Mathematician who might well have been a pupil of Newton or a disciple of Locke. Yet for most men and women life without some sort of faith in the supernatural becomes arid and even alarming; they thus turned from the sardonic skepticism of Voltaire to the delights and solaces of sensibility as offered them by Rousseau. According to Rousseau (whose *Nouvelle Héloïse* was published in 1761) man could only hope to achieve happiness if he abandoned the idea of being clever and sought to become good. He must, with this in mind, develop and exploit a lovely soul, *une belle âme,* which could be acquired only by a "return to nature" and by a rejection of all the artifices and restrictions of this wicked world. He must give free rein to his emotions, cry frequently, be deeply moved to compassion and acutely sensitive to the majesty of nature. Rousseau, whose teaching was continually drenched in tears, *inondé de larmes,* was a crazy genius, gifted with great rhetorical power. His doctrine of sensibility spread throughout the world and filled the vacuum caused by Voltaire's sterile skepticism and by the dry agnosticism of the Encyclopedists and the Paris salons. Even the intellectuals absorbed the fashionable idea that feeling was more important than thought, and it required the emotional and physical excesses of the French Revolution to remind mankind of the importance of balance, reason, and reflection.

SCHILLER

For those of us who admire the achievements of romanticism, it is embarrassing to realize that it was the child of unreason. Politically and socially the man of feeling was certainly a better individual than the man of reason and good taste; but emotionalism in politics can prove a dangerous drug, and the cult of sensibility based on individual experience may lead men to become self-centered and render them miserable by the contrast between their dreams and the facts of existence. Goethe, who in his old age regretted that *Werther* had made so many youths conscious of their own inadequacy, decided that order was preferable to disorder and that learning was a sturdier guide than feeling. He was convinced that the *Sturm und Drang* movement, of which as a young man he had been the leader, had caused more misery than happiness, and most epicureans would agree. One of the most valuable legacies of the romantic movement was that it inculcated a social conscience, a gift of compassion, and that it opened the eyes of man to the beauties of nature and to the comfort that a sensitive appreciation of these beauties can provide.

KEATS

Essentially the romantic movement was a rebellion against convention and an assertion of individualism. Its insistence that all religious dogma and all state institutions were "artificial" produced revolution, agnosticism, and much personal suffering and melancholy. As a political, social, intellectual, and emotional ferment, its effect was destructive in that it weakened faith. But it assuredly enlarged the thinking processes of man and gave to the individual an importance in the scheme of things that he has ever since retained. What today we take for granted as the eternal principles of justice, liberty, and tolerance derives directly from the romantic rebellion. It is therefore pessimistic and incorrect to define its legacy as wholly destructive or negative.

It may have brought melancholy to weak characters and induced much psychological sickness. An emphasis on individualism is apt to render the individual morbidly conscious of his own isolation and inadequacy, until, as with Sören Kierkegaard, he comes to doubt the reality of his own existence. In such defeatist moods the individual may yearn for identification with a group or mass and the protection of some faith and discipline. But to stronger souls the Romantic Revolt brought enlightenment, liberation, self-confidence, and a resolve to develop and express to the uttermost their individual capacities and emotions.

The reliant individual, who was able to master his sensibility, acquired not melancholy and frustration, but an enhanced opportunity for happiness. In the first place, he was liberated from the numbing conviction of original sin, from the sense of unearned guilt, and became convinced that a resolute individual could mold his own destiny. This was a consummate gain. In the second place, it provided him with an almost pantheistic delight in nature, a solace and an enjoyment of which his forebears had been scarcely aware. When I consider the achievements of romanticism, it is not the sickness of the century that I admire, but its vigor.

LAMARTINE

Thus what I reverence in Byron is not the morbidity of *Childe Harold* or the violent rhetoric of *The Giaour,* but the humorous virility of *Don Juan* and his letters, or the final act of self-sacrifice when he left for Greece *"pour finir en héro son immortel ennui."* What I like about Goethe is not the self-distrust of Werther, but the splendid balance of his Olympian old age. Keats in his letters displays a character more resolute and more intelligent than could be suspected from the perusal of his flabbier poems. The strength and vigor of Shelley's philanthropy is not always apparent in his shrill "romantic" paeans. Lamartine to us appears a poet of exaggerated sensibility, and if we admire Hugo for anything more than his mastery of the music of the French language, we admire him for the astounding vigor which he maintained until he was over eighty years of age. I should not desire for one moment to deny or diminish the value of the contribution made to world literature by the Romantic Revolt. I wish only to assert that it is its vigor rather than its sensibility that attracts me, and that the deep gratitude I feel toward it is based on the fact that it enlarged the horizon of my enjoyment by giving me a delight in nature such as the Augustans never provided or possessed.

Who, to my mind, therefore, were the greatest poets that the Romantic Revolt produced? Not Shelley, not Keats, not even my beloved Byron, and certainly not Lamartine or Hugo. But the young Coleridge and the aged Wordsworth. Coleridge taught us the freedom of imagination. It was Wordsworth who taught us to "feel that we are greater than we know" and who preached that only by the worship of natural beauty could mankind achieve "joy in widest commonalty spread." He at least realized that individualism was not enough and that man was but a seedy animal unless he were able to "erect himself" above himself. For Wordsworth the worship of nature was something more than Rousseau's plangent yearning to escape; it was "an active principle," "a grandeur in the beatings of the heart," "a primal sympathy." The intensity of his worship gave him "thoughts that do often lie too deep for tears." Rousseau was incapable of thinking, and his tears were abundant and causeless. Wordsworth has often been reproved for his optimism; yet his was not the vapid optimism of Rousseau, but was based on "the depth, and not the tumult, of the soul," on "man's unconquerable mind," on "spontaneous wisdom breathed by health, truth breathed by cheerfulness." Wordsworth in his mysticism had little sympathy with the materialists and the scientists: he called them "meddling intellects" who "murdered to dissect," and preferred the "heart that watches and receives." His passion for nature was not so much an intellectual as a soothing physical passion:

WORDSWORTH

. . . a sense sublime
Of something far more deeply interfused,
Whose dwelling is the light of setting suns,
And the round ocean and the living air,
And the blue sky, and in the mind of man.

We have all today learned the lesson of Wordsworth and are able in moments of lassitude or despair to solace our fears and to revive our hopes by the sight of wood smoke drifting across a forest or the sound of a blackbird's song. Addison, for all his complacency, never experienced such sedative or stimulating affections. The extent to which the Romantic Revolt expanded the frontier of experience is the measure of its creative achievement. It is to this aspect of the romantic legacy that we today most readily respond.

SCHUBERT

What is so interesting about the Romantic Revolt is that it rapidly infected every aspect of human sensibility and behavior. In music we can trace its stirrings in the genius of Beethoven, its development by Schubert, and finally its cumulating orgy in the operas of Wagner. In painting we have the sudden refusal to accept the classic mode and the replacement of David and Ingres by such younger revolutionaries as Géricault and Delacroix. The latter's *Massacre at Scio* (reproduced on page 75), first exhibited in 1824, the year of Byron's death, caused a sensation. Delacroix was much influenced by Constable's painting and the English artist's abandonment of narrative or historical themes for the simpler realities of nature. It is to the change of feeling and method that Géricault and Delacroix introduced that we owe the rejection of all previous academic standards and the great movements that were thereafter initiated by the impressionists and the postimpressionists. Had it not been for the legacy of Constable and the French romantic painters, art would be a wholly different thing today.

The Romantic Revolt also exercised an immense influence on politics and philosophy. In his fervent reaction against all established institutions and conventions Jean Jacques Rousseau, the prophet of sensibility, preached the doctrine of "natural" rights and taught his generation to love.

How therefore should I define the essential legacy bequeathed to us by the Romantic Revolt? I should define it as *individualism*. The men of the early eighteenth century were obsessed by symmetry, by static rules of order, by established conventions, and by the principles of conduct expected of the several classes or castes of society. It was an artificial century. The romantics destroyed these compartments and insisted that every individual had the right to express his own emotions, to seek his own happiness, and to develop his own capacities, unimpeded by social or prescribed compartments. It is difficult for us to realize how compelling were these social formulas, since they have ceased in this twentieth century to be operative.

EMERSON

I believe that the liberation of human personality, both in life and in art, was the most valuable legacy that the romantics handed down. Admittedly it has its difficulties and its limitations. As was shown by Goethe, Byron, and Chateaubriand, individualism may lead to self-absorption, to despair occasioned by the realization of the gulf that separates the real from the ideal, and to the self-hatred of a Werther, a Childe Harold, or a René. In extreme forms this disease leads to the utter cynicism and self-distrust of such thinkers as Schopenhauer, Nietzsche, and Kierkegaard. But in its healthier form it gives us the solemn optimism of Wordsworth or Emerson and the delight in individual effort manifested by Walt Whitman and the ardent pioneers of our vigorous and ever-changing modern world.

I believe passionately in individualism and even in the cult and exploitation of personality, provided that they retain a social conscience and an aim. For me the legacy of the Romantic Revolt is energy and joy.

One of England's most distinguished men of letters, Sir Harold Nicolson numbers among his many works of criticism and biography a series of studies of some leading figures of the romantic age: Byron, The Last Journey *(1924);* Benjamin Constant *(1949);* Sainte-Beuve *(1957).* He wrote of Voltaire in the March, 1961, HORIZON.

COLLECTION BOURGOGNE–BULLOZ

Byron was still in the nursery when François-René de Chateaubriand, a proud, morose, poetic Breton aristocrat at odds with the French Revolution, took off in 1791 to the wilds of North America to commune with nature and Rousseau's "noble savages." A pioneer in the pursuit of the exotic and primitive, he returned from his reveries along the Mohawk to write travel romances and become by turns a political adventurer, tractarian, diplomat, and recluse whose individuality and high style deeply influenced impressionable French youth. When the admiring Napoleon saw Chateaubriand's portrait painted by Girodet in 1807 (left), he remarked, "He looks like a conspirator who has just come down the chimney."

Best remembered for his *René,* the richly scented tale of a wandering, driven soul that prefigures Byron's *Childe Harold,* he also wrote, as a result of his American immersion, the once-famed romance *Atala* (1801), the improbable story of a Christianized Indian maiden who takes poison rather than violate her vows of chastity. The painter Girodet, whose ideas as to how Indians looked were rather odd, made this the subject of *The Burial of Atala* (below). First shown at the Paris Salon of 1808 to a public fascinated by the faraway, it shows Atala being interred by her Indian lover Chactas (left), with whom she has escaped into what Chateaubriand describes as an Allegheny "desert," and by Father Aubrey, a hermit living there.

LOUVRE–GIRAUDON

Away to Mountains and Meadows

FROM *Waverley Novels*, LONDON 1836

Together with Rousseau's theme of the "noble savage," that of "return to nature" was ever-present in the romantic movement—though the return took many forms and its destinations varied. In France jaded Versailles court ladies, swept away by the new rage of *sensibilité*, had dressed themselves up as milkmaids and fallen into transports over shepherd boys; then came the impulse to seek out such hitherto forbidding retreats as the inner Swiss Alps and the remoter crags of Scotland. Sir Walter Scott, a great traveler of the north, created a virtual cult of Scotland, especially when setting his Waverley Novels there in a twilight atmosphere of historical romance. At left, from *Waverley* itself, is an early illustration depicting the pass of Bally-Brough—"which," proudly says one of Scott's characters, "was kept in former times by ten of the clan Donnochie against a hundred of the Low Country carles."

Not all romantic Englishmen betook themselves that far north or into the past. Yet a revulsion against eighteenth-century urbanity and the veneers of civilization was widespread. Coleridge, saying that we should sink back into a state of childlike wonder, himself was happiest when dreaming in his cottage at Nether Stowey. Wordsworth, after his brief engagement in revolutionary causes, retired to what he wrote of as the "fountains, meadows, hills, and groves" of his beloved Lake Country, making it his very own poetic land while "voyaging on strange seas of thought alone." Among these varied spirits, one of the earthiest was John Constable, who loved the simplicities of hay wains, meadows, homely stiles, and country steeples, and painted them with a warm sense of rediscovered atmosphere of which his 1826 canvas, *The Cornfield* (opposite), is typical.

BY COURTESY OF THE TRUSTEES OF THE NATIONAL GALLERY, LONDON

Romantic Titan and Corsican Ogre

The painter Antoine-Jean Gros was present at the battle of Arcola during Bonaparte's first Italian campaign in 1796 when the fiery young general seized a flag at the disputed bridgehead and led his grenadiers to victory—a moment recorded in the heroic portrait opposite. More than a decade later the Emperor Napoleon, by then arbiter of Europe, gave a far greater painter a very different subject when his legionaries invaded Spain and ruthlessly shot down Madrid patriots. The result was Goya's *Massacre of May 3,* below, one of the most searing indictments ever put on canvas of man's inhumanity to man.

The two paintings illustrate the range of romantic response to the man who was both the movement's most spectacular product and its worst enemy. The insurgent chieftain who had risen from nowhere, Napoleon enthralled romantics who saw him as the embodiment of their ideal of titanic genius and unleashed energy. (He himself remarked of his youth, "I would have fought to the death for Rousseau.") Then, as Europe's cynical despot, he repelled them, although he continued to fascinate them. Creative spirits as varied as Goethe and Beethoven, Byron and Scott, Chateaubriand and Victor Hugo, Stendhal and Manzoni, all at various times fell under his spell.

Goya himself, at the turn of the century a fashionable court painter, had grown so contemptuous of Madrid's encrusted, corrupt aristocracy that he had been inclined to welcome the daemonic Frenchman's intervention in his own country—until the outrages of Napoleon's soldiery aroused him. Chateaubriand, too, turned against the tyrant, yet still praised him as "a poet in action." Beethoven tore up the dedication to the Emperor with which he had prefaced his *Eroica* symphony, but the aura of the unnamed hero's presence still hovers over the work itself. And when, after St. Helena, Napoleon the man was succeeded by Napoleon the myth, the chief agitators for placing him into the pantheon were spokesmen of a new romantic generation, so disenchanted by the dull royalist reaction and grubby self-seeking that followed him that they sought to reconvert the late usurper into a liberating, misunderstood god.

PRADO—SCALA

LOUVRE—GIRAUDON

BY COURTESY OF THE TRUSTEES OF THE TATE GALLERY, LONDON

KUNSTHAUS, ZURICH

The Farther Shores of Vision

In encouraging limitless expression of self, the romantic movement gave voice also to extreme individualists whose predilections ran to the mystical, the fantastic, and the mysterious. Three such figures—diverse in aim, yet united by apartness and introspection, and strange men all—were the artists whose work is shown here: the English visionary, William Blake (1757–1827), represented (above left) by his illustration to the *Inferno* showing Dante and Virgil at the entrance to Hell; the Swiss pursuer of grotesque and macabre themes, Henry Fuseli (1741–1825), represented by his *Midsummer Night's Dream* (above right) based on Shakespeare's comedy; and the German apostle of self-immersion in dreamlike scenery, Caspar David Friedrich (1774–1840), creator of a long line of haunting canvases such as his *Chalk Cliffs at Rügen* (opposite).

Blake, a rapt oddity and recluse from the glitter of late Georgian England, was sometimes thought insane, sometimes just simple. He was obviously innocent of many of the canons of accomplished art, as his anatomically vague figures floating about like phantoms show. Convention and correctness meant nothing to him; he was even so careless, when inscribing the most famous single line of Dante above his drawing, as to misquote it: he should have written, *"Lasciate ogni speranza, voi ch'entrate."* Yet his strangely-drawn shapes reflect the inspiration of a seer whose art was as personal as his deep religious devotion, and who (misquoting Dante or not) was also a major poet in his own right.

One of Blake's few close friends was the Swiss Fuseli, a man of diametrically contrasting tastes who lived for many years in England. A Zurich artist's son raised to be a Lutheran pastor, Fuseli rebelled against his appointed destiny and became a painter of pronounced erotic and diabolic bent instead. Distortion, perversity, and exploration of the murky layers of the improbable and repulsive became his signature on canvas—as in this sardonic one, which recounts the moment when Shakespeare's fairy queen Titania, awakening amid the trance into which her kingly husband Oberon has magically cast her, fawns amorously over the humble weaver Bottom, who is masked in an ass's head.

Friedrich, for his part, was a rare and seeking spirit of yet another stripe. Born in Pomerania as the son of a humble soap-boiler, he grew up to be seized by the whole array of romantic passions that were exercising the still-fragmented Germany of his day—the *Weltschmerz* of Goethe's lovelorn young hero Werther; the cult of *Sehnsucht* (i.e., dreamlike longing—usually for the unattainable); and the drive toward German nationhood, which involved turning against hitherto dominant formal French taste and rediscovering the lure of the German wild. All these urges Friedrich pursued—as painter, nationalist poet, and mystic in love with Gothic ruins, myths, bare churchyards, and gnarled Teutonic trees—finally to fall into insanity. One of the happier of his brooding works is the one opposite, which is thought to portray the painter himself (somewhat clumsily postured at center), his bride, and his brother-in-law, all peering down from the chalky heights of the Baltic island of Rügen into the silence and the sea beyond.

LOUVRE–GIRAUDON

Passion at its Most Visible

In his self-portrait, above, Eugène Delacroix tells us succinctly what sort of a man he was: the intense vision, the ardent spirit that he fed with prodigious energies, the hauteur that served his need of independence and added glamour to his attractive presence—it is all there. Here is the man and the artist whom Baudelaire described as "passionately in love with passion, and coldly determined to find ways of expressing passion in the most visible manner."

Physically Delacroix was not strong; he was febrile and often ill, but he was also indefatigable. "I can work without stopping," he once wrote, "and without hope of reward"; and this is what he did by and large. During his lifetime he became a symbol of freedom and revolution in the arts, understood by only a few admirers. But with massive will he pursued his personal vision to heights approached by none of his romantic contemporaries in painting.

Delacroix became obsessed by the expressive power of pigment. The audacity with which he juxtaposed broad strokes of primary colors led his detractors to ridicule him for using a "drunken broom" for a brush. His first large masterpiece, *The Massacre at Scio* (opposite), was publicly shown in 1824, the year Lord Byron lost his life in the cause of Greek independence. This scene, recalling the barbarism with which the Turks decimated the innocent population of the Aegean island of Scio (Chios), had an immediate claim on public sympathy. But at the Academy it caused only scandal. The painting was still wet when it was hung. Just before the exhibition opened, Delacroix had seen for the first time John Constable's famous *Hay Wain,* and it had been for him a transforming revelation. Inspired by the freshness and freedom of the Englishman's work, he hastily repainted his own canvas to heighten its effect. Even Antoine-Jean Gros, one academician who had supported Delacroix, was dismayed by the passages of fragmented strong color with which the canvas was loaded. To the delight of critics, Gros dubbed it the "massacre of painting."

Three years later an even greater scandal followed the showing of Delacroix's most voluptuous and colorful picture, *The Death of Sardanapalus* (pages 76–77). Here again the theme was timely enough. The romantic vogue for Orientalism was running strong. Byron had dealt with this epic story of the Assyrian king who, threatened with death at the hands of his generals, had his harem, his slaves, his dogs, and his horses slaughtered in his presence before they all burned on his own funeral pyre. But even Delacroix's friends would not accept the "confused" composition, the "unfinished" drawing, the unrestrained opulence of the painting.

Actually Delacroix was one of the best draftsmen of his day. There was nothing random or whimsical about his composition or his definition of form and space. He rejected the undisciplined emotional profligacy we associate with romanticism and put his theories to work with the most deliberate calculation. The upheavals he caused in Salon circles were the price French painting had to pay for its vital renewal. History calls Delacroix the leader of the romantic artists, but with the intense individualism of the true romantic he disdained to be classified as a romantic. He was, in fact, closer to the great tradition of European painting than most of his contemporaries—closer to Rubens, Titian, Veronese, Ruisdael, and other titans of the past, and to men like Cézanne, Renoir, and Van Gogh to come.

The determining experience of Delacroix's life came in 1832, when he made a memorable trip to Morocco. The innumerable sketches and notes he recorded during this journey served him as a source book for the rest of his life. Two years before his death he drew upon them for *The Lion Hunt* (pages 78–79), one of his most typical paintings, full of the violence, exoticism, and the magical color that came so compulsively from his fastidiously controlled brush. But whether he painted snarling lions and dashing Arab horsemen or romances set in the Middle Ages, as in *The Abduction of Rebecca* from Scott's *Ivanhoe* (cover), Delacroix was searching for symbols of universal passions.

The intelligence, urbanity, and integrity that made Delacroix a revolutionary in his studio endeared him as a person to the most cultivated minds of his day. Baudelaire, Gautier, Balzac, Dumas *père*, Chopin, and George Sand were among those who welcomed him to their conversational circles. Upon his death in 1863, Baudelaire wrote his eulogy. "What is this mysterious *je ne sais quoi* which Delacroix, to the glory of our century, has translated better than any other artist?" he asked. "It is the indivisible, the impalpable; it is the dream, the nerves, the *soul*. And he has done this . . . with no other means save contour and color. He has done it better than anyone else. . . ."

On The Following Pages: PAINTINGS BY DELACROIX

Opposite: THE MASSACRE AT SCIO (1824)

Pages 76–77: THE DEATH OF SARDANAPALUS (1828)

Pages 78–79: THE LION HUNT (1861)

Page 80: GEORGE SAND (1838)

LOUVRE; COURTESY *Life*

LOUVRE–GIRAUDON

WALLACE KIRKLAND–ART INSTITUTE OF CHICAGO

MALERISAMLINGEN ORDRUPGAARD, COPENHAGEN; COURTESY *Life*

LOUVRE–GIRAUDON

At the height of their love affair, the poet Alfred de Musset sketched this image of George Sand and his wild-haired self.

PRIVATE COLLECTION–GIRAUDON

Inamorata of the Age

When Delacroix in 1838 painted the unfinished portrait at left of George Sand, it was part of a canvas on the other half of which he depicted Frédéric Chopin, then her great love. As if recalling the manner in which all her tumultuous affairs of passion ended, the canvas itself was torn apart—precisely when is not known, but certainly after the artist's death—and the Chopin half of it (above left) now hangs in the Louvre.

An earlier romantic generation had its *femme fatale* in Mme de Staël (1766–1817), the well-born rebel, amorist, oracle, and nonstop talker beloved by Benjamin Constant and many others, and feared for her cutting prose by Napoleon himself. The second generation found itself with an even more fatal presence in Amandine-Aurore-Lucie Dupin, the super-amorist and total emancipator of emotions who is remembered not under her married name of Mme Dudevant but under the masculine literary one she assumed for a lifetime of nonstop writing and unfettered love.

Like Mme de Staël, George Sand (1804–1876) was not particularly seductive in appearance, and her femininity was not furthered by her habit of smoking pipes and cigars. Yet she enthralled a long line of impressionable and creative men of whom the most famous, next to Chopin, was the handsome and devastating young poet Alfred de Musset, who preceded him by some years in her affections and whose sketch of himself and her together appears above at right.

Reared on a Norman estate, laying claim both to royal blood in her veins (through an ancestral illegitimate connection with Louis XV) and to being "a daughter of the people," she was precociously brilliant and overthrew an early, tawdry marriage to erupt in tractarian novels calling for liberation from the conjugal tie. She insisted upon free pursuit of love; yet her own impulses were so headstrong and masterful that she needed to dominate her lovers, with the result that she sought out gifted but highly sensitive spirits whom she then proceeded to "mother"—until she wearied or they rebelled.

Two such spirits were Musset and Chopin—the first, despite his dashing appearance in sky-blue clothes and his successes in many boudoirs, a tormented man given to drink, whom she nursed through delirium in Venice; the second, deep in illness and depression when she almost literally carried him off to refuge in Majorca. In both instances great love ended in great revulsion and in more autobiographical novels on her part: books (some forty in all) which she wrote at such feverish pace, spending night after night at her desk producing them, that her lover Musset called her *"une terrible vache à écrire"*—"a terrible literary cow."

Franz Liszt, another of her admirers, sardonically described her method with men thus: "[She] catches her butterfly and tames it in her cage by feeding it on flowers and nectar—that is the love period. Then she sticks her pin into it when it struggles. . . . After that she vivisects it, stuffs it, and adds it to her collection of heroes for novels." Yet the poet Heinrich Heine, who also admired her, gives a warmer first-hand picture of her in the years when she inspired Chopin to some of his finest work: "*She*—beautiful auburn hair falling to her shoulders; eyes rather lusterless and sleepy, but calm and gentle; a smile of great good nature. . . . *He*—endowed with abnormal sensitiveness which the least contact can wound . . . a man made for intimacies, withdrawn into a mysterious world of his own, from which he sometimes emerges in a sudden spate of violent, charming, and fantastic speech."

Altogether an amazing woman: though many scoffed at her, Balzac and Dostoevsky both acclaimed her as a literary master, the sage Victorian Matthew Arnold respectfully visited her, and Gustave Flaubert wept at the news of her death.

BIBLIOTHEQUE OPERA—GIRAUDON

The Wild Men of 1830

Rebellion against staid reaction in France after Napoleon's fall brought out small armies of young writers, artists, and students under the banner of "*Romantisme*," along with two new standard-bearers, Hector Berlioz (right, in a portrait by Courbet) and Victor Hugo (opposite, as etched by Achille Deveria). Both were men of the new century, born in 1803 and 1802, respectively; both were explosive, virile, egocentric spirits out to make short shrift of the conventions; and both attained their first scandalizing successes in the revolutionary year 1830. Berlioz's was the *Symphonie Fantastique*, a ferocious work, ending upon a witches' carnival, that led him on to orchestral excesses of which the German cartoon above is a contemporary caricature. Hugo's success that year was his poetic drama *Hernani*, so insurgent in style and content that it caused nightly near-riots at the Comédie Française. At the top of the opposite page, such an eruption during its closing scene —the double suicide of the lovers—is cartooned by Granville.

Berlioz claimed Beethoven as his master, yet he himself more resembled the taste

LOUVRE

PHOTOGRAPHS BIBLIOTHEQUE NATIONALE–GIRAUDON

of the future Richard Wagner in his urge musically to tell a story (preferably a strange and bloody one), to make music itself a dramatic spectacle, and to achieve new, stupendous instrumental effects—even, in the case of the *Symphonie funèbre et triomphale,* having a cannon go off.

Hugo, later to be more prized as poet and novelist than as playwright, broke from the classic French theater, with its rigidities of place, time, and faultless formal verse, to emulate what many Frenchmen still deplored as the wild "Gothic" dramas of Shakespeare. This his free-form *Hernani* did, throwing the gauntlet to conservatives so boldly that they rose up to pitch it out of the nation's theater as an outrage. Hugo, however, surrounded himself with a claque of young supporters—some long-haired and bearded or garbed strangely, like Théophile Gautier in his rose-colored jacket and green trousers—to outshout and indeed outfight the "baldheads" at each performance. Thus defended, *Hernani* ran for a record forty-five nights at the Comédie, and "*Romantisme*" won a decisive victory.

The Spell of the Master

The master at the piano here is the young virtuoso and composer Franz Liszt; the greater master whose bust faces him is, of course, Ludwig van Beethoven. Behind Liszt in this retrospective canvas painted by Joseph Danhauser in 1840 are grouped some of the greatest celebrities of the romantic age—all virtuosos in their fields in a time that encouraged breathtaking performance. Closest to him sits George Sand; beside her is Alexandre Dumas, the astoundingly prolific author of plays and melodramatic romances. Behind her, left to right, stand Victor Hugo; the wizard violinist Paganini, who first amazed Europe in 1805 with his almost unbelievable dexterity; and the composer Rossini, who in eight fabulous years wrote twenty operas, culminating in *William Tell*—and then wrote no more. Reclining at Liszt's side is the Comtesse Marie d'Agoult, who was one of his great loves in the ardent years before he took on the habit of a Franciscan abbé, and who bore him three children—one of them, Cosima, to become the wife of Richard Wagner.

Beethoven, although by then totally deaf, had done Liszt the honor of coming to attend his playing in Vienna as a twelve-year-old prodigy, and Liszt went on performing the revered master's works with lifelong devotion. His own music, however, ultra-rhapsodic and often out to achieve bombastic effects, was of quite another order. As for Beethoven, though he became as highly prized by romantic musicians as Byron was by poets, his own sympathies did not lie with romantic extremes. "Emotional displays are fit only for women," he once remarked (to a woman). "In a man, music should strike fire from his spirit." This his own imperishably did. Classic in musical form yet spacious in feeling, he sought in it to identify his own personal sorrows, loves, and hopes with those of all mankind—never more greatly than in the mighty hymn to brotherhood based on Schiller's "Ode to Joy" that dominates the final movement of his last symphony. Of this the opening bars, as sketched in his first draft, appear at right.

INSTITUTE TREUHANDVERWALTUNG VON KULTURGUT, MUNICH-KEMPTER

OVERLEAF: *Climax of New Hope*

As in letters and the arts, romantic fervor could be said to have reached its peak also in the political sphere in the year 1830, the "July Days" of which in France saw an uprising that has been called the most intellectual of revolutions. Amid Paris street battles in which barricades were thrown up and defended by working men and scholars alike, the repressive Bourbon monarchy was thrown out. It was hoped by men ranging from Lamartine to Hugo that by bringing in the Duc d'Orléans, son of a regicide and revolutionary fighter at Valmy, the national inspiration which had fired France under the tricolor of Napoleon at his best could be restored. The engraving on the following pages by Garneray depicts the climactic moment in July when fraternizing troops and rebels mass before the Paris Hôtel de Ville to acclaim the aged Marquis de Lafayette of revolutionary fame as he appears on the center balcony to embrace the Duke, who is waving the *drapeau* and who is soon to be proclaimed Louis-Philippe, King of the French.

MUSÉE CARNAVALET, PARIS

BY COURTESY OF THE TRUSTEES OF THE NATIONAL GALLERY, LONDON

Enter the Machine

The Romantic Revolt came in to the sound of sighs and went out to that of steam engines; it was submerged under the grime of the Industrial Revolution. Symbolic of what was ahead is the approaching locomotive in J. M. W. Turner's *Rain, Steam and Speed,* painted in 1844 at the height of the railway craze in England. It shows a Great Western Railway train crossing the Taplow-Maidenhead viaduct. Intent on atmospheric effects, Turner viewed the scene romantically; yet within a few decades whole English counties would be overhung with smoke, as visions of a boundless future became transformed into a world of productive but dark and prosaic factories.

The Outrageous IONESCO

Owing something to Kafka but more to Marx (the Brothers, not Karl), his plays are startling, often hilarious, and almost always bewildering. Is he talking nonsense or offering a meaningful comment on life? Here is an interview with Europe's most debated playwright —along with a sample of his recent work

No dramatist of our time is more bizarre in method and enigmatic in meaning than Eugène Ionesco, the eruptive Parisian whose work was known in America only to very small off-Broadway audiences until his *Rhinoceros* opened in New York last winter to major critical acclaim. Within a few months he has become as hotly debated here as he has been for some time abroad, and is regarded alternatively as sheer prankster and comic philosopher. The interview that follows, conducted in French, took place on the occasion of Ionesco's first visit to New York shortly before the opening of his surprising hit.

Ionesco is forty-eight, born in Rumania, the only son of a French mother and Rumanian father. His early years were spent in France. He was living in Rumania when the Iron Guard began to gain power, and like his hero Bérenger in *Rhinoceros,* he felt that he couldn't give in to the rise of the cult. He left his job—he was teaching French in a *lycée* —and took his bride of some months back to France, where he started working toward a doctorate in French letters. His love of language, his bizarre manipulation of it, is one of the salient characteristics of his art. He has a predilection for puns and word games, and each of his plays is animated by the poetic power of ambiguity, not only in the action of his characters but also in the meaning of the words they use.

There are thirteen plays, of which the first—presented in 1950—was *The Bald Soprano.* They bear equivocal designations—comic drama, tragic farce, pseudo drama—and with them Ionesco is often said to have evolved a new theatrical genre: the metaphysical farce, a twentieth-century morality play which does not preach.

The literary ancestors of this genre are the surrealists, the symbolists, the Dadaists, and, in particular, an *enfant terrible* named Alfred Jarry who wrote the first metaphysical farce, *Ubu Roi,* while he was still in school. It was performed in 1896. In this raucous play there appears for the first time, practiced by a character called Père Ubu, a science called 'Pataphysics—a mock philosophy in which Ionesco is deeply interested. It has been described as "the science of the realm beyond metaphysics." In 1948 Jarry's followers honored his invention of the science by creating the College of 'Pataphysics. It is an august body with a publication of its own,

By ROSETTE LAMONT

Cahiers du Collège de 'Pataphysique, and an absurdly involved hierarchy of rulers and commissions under the supervision of a Vice-Curator, six Proveditors-General, officials of the Rogation and Executive Organon, and a Corps of Satraps. The College is actually a spoof on all academies, existing forms of government, and official bodies, with particular emphasis on such trappings as honors, processionals, decorations, and titles. Ionesco claims he is very proud of belonging to the group and of being honored with the title of Satrap. Other Satraps include Raymond Queneau, author of the best seller *Zazie dans le métro;* the film director René Clair; and the artists Marcel Duchamp and Jean Dubuffet (the latter enjoys the coincidental distinction of having the progenitor Ubu embodied in his own name).

Ionesco's view of the world is by no means as flippant as might be suggested by his association with the College. His plays often seem to have been written only to amuse by their clever twists of situation and language; but even a short conversation with Ionesco reveals his fundamental seriousness. His demeanor is serious, his voice slow and measured —but then suddenly one is aware of the duality: he smiles, a quick childlike smile revealing teeth the size of milk teeth; the hair at the sides of his head is usually long, surrounding his face with a fringe, like a parted stage curtain, from which he peers out, wary and amused.

IONESCO: If I don't answer your questions right away, you mustn't mind me. Any constructive thinking one does is done at the rate of an hour per month, and the rest of the time we exploit what we have achieved in this hour of grace. At the end of two weeks the substance is drained, and we utter only stupidities.

INTERVIEWER: Let me start with a factual question, then. You have been known as a dramatist for only the last ten years. Your first play, *The Bald Soprano,* was presented in 1950. What kind of work did you do before that time?

IONESCO: Employee in a publishing firm, teacher, journalist, laborer, unemployed intellectual, scholarship student in the keep of the French government, white-collar worker, bureaucrat.

INTERVIEWER: Did you ever write a play before *The Bald Soprano?*

IONESCO: I wrote my first play at the age of eleven. It was a patriotic play.

INTERVIEWER: When were you conscious of having become a writer?

IONESCO: I am less conscious of having become a writer than a businessman. I spend the greater part of my time calling people and receiving calls, signing contracts, fighting with my agents, running to my lawyer. For this activity, which takes a lot of my time, I've had to engage a secretary. My typist used to be a nice old lady. Now it's a bearded young man. But you know, there's something pleasant about all this fussing around. At a time of sterility, such as now, after I've dictated six or seven letters, spoken to a journalist, given a lecture, I've done nothing, but at least I have the feeling I've worked.

INTERVIEWER: Do you write every day?

IONESCO: In principle, yes. Actually, no.

INTERVIEWER: But I am speaking of a creative period in your life.

IONESCO: For some time now I have decided I ought to work every day, so I do, even if it's only for five minutes.

INTERVIEWER: How do you and your secretary work together?

IONESCO: I dictate. If I'm not satisfied with what I have dictated, I use the text as a rough draft for future dictation. Sometimes I make things up on the spur of the moment, and at other times I come with a written text to use as a point of reference. Sometimes I write something at home and come with it all ready for dictation. As you see, it varies a great deal.

INTERVIEWER: Do you dictate your plays because you like to hear the way a line sounds—test it out, so to speak?

IONESCO: I wish I could say that. Actually it's because I'm far too lazy to write. I can't sit down at a table any longer. The idea of picking up a pen and writing sickens me.

INTERVIEWER: What about typing? Do you ever sit down at a typewriter to write?

IONESCO: Yes, all the time. I sit down at the typewriter, and then I don't write because I can't type.

INTERVIEWER: What about the creative act itself?

IONESCO: I used to have to walk, now I sleep. Many people get their best ideas at that moment in the morning between sleep and waking. I get up and write down as many thoughts as I can. However, it's become increasingly difficult. Ideas seem to flee from me. When I stand motionless, they take to their heels. When I'm lying down, I feel that today things will work out, but as soon as I get out of bed my ideas fall at my feet like broken pitchers. Nothing at all remains.

INTERVIEWER: What appears in your mind first: an image, a character, a situation, a word?

IONESCO: It used to be a line of dialogue, as in cartoons or comic strips. You see a character saying something, and what he says appears as the caption. And so I used to see first the written words, then the character speaking these words, then the complete picture, and it would all tie up neatly. Now all this has changed. I write with great difficulty. It takes me months and months to finish a play. Sometimes the act of writing seems meaningless to me now, absolutely meaningless.

INTERVIEWER: What you are saying reminds me that some people claim you were happier when you were less successful, when your audience was made up of three or four good friends, your wife, and your daughter.

IONESCO: It's true that I feel that the struggle is over. Maybe I'm just getting old and weary. But of course one has to earn a living.

INTERVIEWER: How did success come to you?

IONESCO: Raymond Queneau, the nov-

Another in the HORIZON interview series THE ARTIST SPEAKS FOR HIMSELF under the editorship of George Plimpton

---

elist, helped me a great deal. He came to see my play *The Bald Soprano.* It was being given in a tiny theater, Le Théâtre des Noctambules. Queneau had just published his *Exercices de style,* and he understood perfectly the kind of word game I used in my play. He liked it, and the next day he brought Armand Salacrou, the dramatist, and later Jean Paulhan and some others. Then at a cocktail party at Gallimard, where he worked at the time, he posted himself at the door and told every one of the two hundred guests: "Did you see Ionesco's *The Bald Soprano*? Well, you must." No one had heard of Ionesco, but that's how it started.

INTERVIEWER: Did any other French writer help you in starting?

IONESCO: Yes, Jean Anouilh. By writing an article in *Le Figaro* the day before *The Chairs* was supposed to close. He gave me quite a build-up. Now he doesn't like me and Beckett. I guess we've become too successful to be safe.

INTERVIEWER: What about the title of your first play, *The Bald Soprano*? After all, there is no bald soprano in the play.

IONESCO: That's precisely the point. Actually, the title used to be *English Without Toil,* because I derived the whole idea for the play from a conversation text by that name, the Assimil method. At one time I wanted to learn English, and though, as you can see, I never succeeded, I became fascinated with this textbook. In it you meet a number of people—Mr. and Mrs. Smith, Mr. Martin—and all of them seem amazed at their own existence. They have the need to explain the simplest things, such as where they are, what they like to eat, who is married to whom. I decided to put these characters on the stage. People misunderstood my intention; they assumed I was laughing at the bourgeoisie, whereas I was trying to evolve a free, pure comic style similar to that of the Marx Brothers in the movies.

INTERVIEWER: But this still doesn't explain the title.

IONESCO: That's a well-known story, and I've told it many times. It happened by pure accident. Nicolas Bataille, my director, did not like the original title. During a rehearsal one of the actors flubbed his lines. In the text I had something about a blond soprano, but he said "bald soprano." We all laughed, and the mistake became the title of the play. Of course, we also changed the reference within the play. This made it even wilder—which is exactly what I was aiming for.

INTERVIEWER: Would you say that *The Lesson* and *The Chairs* still belong to your first period?

IONESCO: I would say that three plays belong to my first manner: *The Bald Soprano, The Lesson,* and *Jack.* These three plays were exercises. I wanted to set in motion the mechanism of the theater. I was trying to depict the progression of an aimless passion. In *The Lesson,* for example, comedy changes to tragedy. The play is a ceremonial of murder. It was in this play that I became conscious of dramatic structure.

INTERVIEWER: Were you aiming for a kind of purity of style?

IONESCO: I wanted to divest the theatrical language of its literary aspects. Like the cubist painters, I wished to find the joints of my art and show them in motion.

INTERVIEWER: But what about *The Chairs*? Does that play belong to the same period?

IONESCO: No. In *The Chairs* I tried for a kind of amplification. Objects themselves became a language. I wanted to find a visual language, a language of the stage more direct, more shocking, and stronger than that of words. You see, the artist is seldom able to renew literary themes. There are few new themes. What he can do is renew language.

INTERVIEWER: What about *Rhinoceros*? It is, after all, a much more traditional kind of play.

IONESCO: That's true. This does not mean I'm going to keep on writing this way, but everyone assumes as much. All the people who were once my enemies are now welcoming me into the fold, and my friends have turned against me. My friends want me to remain true to myself, and by that they mean that I have no right to change.

INTERVIEWER: Are you thinking of a play right now?

IONESCO: I've been thinking for some time of a play in which I would speak of death. I wish to describe the agony of a dying man. I am thinking of putting on the stage a dying king. This monarch might represent perishing modern values. So many things go through my mind when I read the papers, and I get annoyed by what I read. Somehow it has all crystallized round a central theme, that of death, of the agony of a king. Yet at the same time I don't seem to be able to come to grips with my subject. Perhaps it is because this is the deepest, the greatest anguish of my being, and there is a kind of psychic refusal.

INTERVIEWER: Haven't you already treated the theme of death in *The Killer*?

IONESCO: The theme of *The Killer* is evil, fundamental aggressiveness without reason, almost without hatred. A kind of divine principle of destruction.

INTERVIEWER: You use the same hero in *The Killer* and in *Rhinoceros*—Bérenger, a modest, frightened, yet courageous man.

IONESCO: He is the hero in spite of himself. He's terribly frightened, but he says to himself that no one seems to be doing anything, and that someone *has* to do something, even if that someone is as insignificant as himself. He has the feeling that he is struggling against the whole world, that he alone can save the world. Of course he knows all along that it isn't so, but he acts as though it were.

INTERVIEWER: Is Bérenger an aspect of yourself?

IONESCO: I suppose so. When I was in Rumania as an adolescent I witnessed the rise of fascism. Everyone around me joined the Iron Guard. Everyone except me. Somehow, I did not espouse the reigning ideology. To this day I still don't know how it happened. All I know is that I was quite alone. It took twenty years for that to appear in a play.

INTERVIEWER: Is *Rhinoceros* then

INTERVIEW CONTINUED ON PAGE 93

Improvisation, or The Shepherd's Chameleon

A One-Act Play by EUGÈNE IONESCO

The earmarks of an Ionesco play are its deliberately banal dialogue, dead-pan logic, and wayward humor, but the distinctive flavor of this compound is not so readily described. To convey some idea of it, one has to fall back on the author's own words. Beginning on this page is a portion of his Improvisation, or The Shepherd's Chameleon, *a satire on critics and, for all one knows—since one of the characters is named Ionesco—on playwrights. When this short play was presented one afternoon last fall in the Matinee Theatre Series of the Greater New York Chapter of ANTA, the author attended. The resulting situation, with one Ionesco (real) in the audience and another Ionesco (counterfeit) on the stage, was no more intricate than the opening of the play itself, which is like a set of lunatic Chinese boxes. The other characters are three virtually identical critics called Bartholomeus I, II, and III, and a charwoman, Marie. This excerpt, in a translation by Donald Watson, is reprinted from Eugène Ionesco's* The Killer and Other Plays, *published by Grove Press, Inc.*

IONESCO *is asleep, his head on the table, surrounded with books and manuscripts. A ball-point pencil is sticking out of one hand. A bell rings.* IONESCO *snores. It rings again and then there is the sound of beating on the door and cries of: "Ionesco! Ionesco!" Finally* IONESCO *jumps and rubs his eyes.*

MAN'S VOICE: Ionesco! Are you there?

IONESCO: Yes . . . Just a second! . . . What's the matter now? [*Smoothing his untidy hair* IONESCO *goes to the door and opens it.* BARTHOLOMEUS I *appears, in a scholar's gown.*]

BART I: Morning, Ionesco.

IONESCO: Morning, Bartholomeus.

BART I: Glad I've found you in! I damned nearly went away and I'd have been very angry, specially as you haven't a phone . . . What on earth were you doing?

IONESCO: I was working, working . . . I was writing!

BART I: The new play? Is it ready? I'm waiting for it.

IONESCO: [*sitting in his armchair and motioning* BARTHOLOMEUS *to a chair*] Sit down. [BARTHOLOMEUS *sits.*] Well, I'm working on it, you know. I've got right down to it. I feel quite overworked. It's coming along, but it's not easy. It's got to be perfect, hasn't it? No repetition, no dull passages . . . So you see I'm tightening, tightening it up . . .

BART I: You *have* finished it, then? . . . The first draft, let's see that . . .

IONESCO: But I tell you I'm still tightening the dialogue . . .

BART I: Do I understand you're tightening the dialogue before you've finished the play? I suppose that's *one* way of writing.

IONESCO: It's *my* way.

BART I: Now listen, have you finished the play or haven't you?

IONESCO: [*hunting amongst his papers on the table*] Yes . . . well no, you see . . . not exactly. It's here, of course, but I can't read it to you in its present state . . . so long as it's not . . .

BART I: . . . finished . . . polished off! . . .

IONESCO: No, no . . . not polished off . . . polished, perfect! It's not the same thing at all.

BART I: Pity. We're going to miss a good chance. I've had a very interesting offer. A theater that's dead keen on having one of your plays. The directors want it at once. They've asked me to take the job on and produce it according to the latest dramatic theories. Theories worthy of a people's theater in this ultrascientific age we live in. They'll bear all the costs, publicity and so on, providing the cast's limited to four or five and it won't cost too much to mount . . .

IONESCO: Tell them to be patient for a day or two. I promise I'll have tightened it all up by then—though, it's true, the season *is* getting on.

BART I: So long as the *play* is, we can still fix it up . . .

IONESCO: Which theater is it?

BART I: A new theater, with a scientific director and a young company of scientific actors who want to launch out with *you.* You'll get scientific treatment. The auditorium's not too big, seats for twenty-five and standing room for four . . . It's for a people's audience, but a select one.

IONESCO: Not too bad. If only we could fill it every evening!

BART I: Half fill it, even, and I'd be satisfied . . . Anyway, they want to start at once.

IONESCO: That'd be fine, if only the play was absolutely ready . . .

BART I: But you say it's practically all written!

IONESCO: Yes . . . yes . . . it is *practically* all written!

BART I: What's it all about? What's it called?

IONESCO: [*embarrassed and rather conceited*] Er . . . what's it about? . . . You want to know what it's about? . . . And what it's called? . . . Er . . . you know I never know how to talk about my plays . . . It's all in the dialogue, in the acting, in the stage effects, it's very visual, as usual . . . With me there's always first some image, some line or other which sets off the creative mechanism. And then I just let my own characters carry me along, I never know exactly where

COPYRIGHT © BY JOHN CALDER (PUBLISHERS) LTD. 1960

PLAY CONTINUED ON PAGE 94

INTERVIEW CONTINUED FROM PAGE 91

concerned with the individual's struggle against a rising political ideology?

IONESCO: It is wider than that. It depicts a struggle against any tyrannical and dogmatic system, any ideology that becomes an idolatry, be it of East or West. It makes the Brechtians quite mad. I don't care for didactic theater. The theater is an autonomous system of expression. It cannot be the illustration of an ideology. Anyway, all affirmations are stupid. Only second-class minds, grade-B intellectuals, make violent affirmations.

INTERVIEWER: Would you name one such intellectual among your contemporaries?

IONESCO: Sartre. He's a superior kind of fool. Like most intellectuals he gives in to brute force, he admires it. First he reads Heidegger and Husserl and becomes their disciple. Why? Because at that time Germany is a strong country, and political power gets confused in his mind with cultural vitality. Then, after the defeat of Germany, he becomes a humanist and an existentialist. Now, existentialism was at its beginning a philosophy of the absurd; how can it become humanistic? Still, that's the way the wind blows. Then Russia becomes powerful. So of course Sartre turns Marxist. Marxism is a religion, a mystique. And yet Sartre the intellectual, the clear, lucid mind, takes up the cult. I believe that Sartre's ideology, his noble sentiments, spring from envy and jealousy. He wants to speak to Khrushchev; he goes to Brazil to attack De Gaulle—what does it all mean? Spite. Sartre would like to be a politician or at least a diplomat. His is the case of a lost vocation.

INTERVIEWER: Doesn't he think of himself as a kind of lucid conscience in the world, a guiding prophet?

IONESCO: Exactly—except that he's shortsighted and timid. Like all timid people he gives in to the power of historical events. Then he flies to the rescue of history. What is interesting in a man is not to know *what* he thinks, but to discover *why* he thinks what he thinks. Sartre is motivated by self-hatred. Most French intellectuals nowadays are masochists. They hate French nationalism, and yet they worship all nationalistic feelings which are not French. They all hate Malraux, who's the best of them all. They hate him because he has a cabinet post. In fact, when at the end of the first performance of *Rhinoceros* I was called out on the stage and saluted Malraux, who was sitting in his box, I was denounced bitterly. *I* was called a rhinoceros myself for making this gesture.

INTERVIEWER: What do you think of De Gaulle?

IONESCO: I think he is an admirable, lonely man who wants to save France.

INTERVIEWER: And the French intellectuals are fascinated by Khrushchev?

IONESCO: They are. You cannot imagine how excited everyone got over his shoe. When he took off his shoe at the United Nations General Assembly and started banging on the table with it, I felt as though his shoe were on *my* table, as though he were insulting me personally, but the French intellectuals were delighted. Their suspicion of the United States, its philanthropy, is to my mind one of the greatest injustices of history.

INTERVIEWER: What do you think of Arthur Adamov, who writes in the same vein as you do but is a leftist writer and a great admirer of Brecht?

IONESCO: We used to be great friends till my plays caught on. Adamov was present at a performance of *The Chairs* when there were three or four people in the audience. He was wild with excitement. He paced the room, waved his arms, said it was magnificent. Empty seats on the stage, empty seats in the theater. *"Ça a de la gueule!"* he shouted. As soon as I became a little more successful, he became my bitter enemy. As for his political ideology—which is as shifty as any I have ever known—I've always thought it an effect of his disappointments as a writer.

INTERVIEWER: Do you like his plays?

IONESCO: Yes. I particularly like the early ones, *La Parodie* and *Le Professeur Taranne*.

INTERVIEWER: And Camus, did you know him?

IONESCO: Poor Camus. We became friends about five months before he died. Before that he did not like me very much. He didn't consider that I took life too seriously. But shortly before his death he spoke of one of my plays over the radio. I was in the theater rehearsing *Rhinoceros* the day he died. Someone called out Barrault and told him, and then Barrault walked out on the stage and told us. Simone Valère started crying, and the rehearsal was stopped. Then Barrault ordered the rehearsal to go on after fifteen minutes. The following day, however, he could not show up.

INTERVIEWER: People have called Camus's death absurd.

IONESCO: That is stupid. The only absurd thing is life itself.

INTERVIEWER: Some people say that you criticize the bourgeoisie in your plays, while others call you a bourgeois writer. Which are you?

IONESCO: That is the reason of my visit to the United States. I have come on a secret mission, which is to rehabilitate the bourgeoisie.

INTERVIEWER: This does not seem to go together with your membership in the Collège de 'Pataphysique. How do you reconcile the two?

IONESCO: One can say anything about 'Pataphysics. Everything is true.

INTERVIEWER: What is the Collège de 'Pataphysique?

IONESCO: It's a club.

INTERVIEWER: Is the whole thing a big practical joke?

IONESCO: Oh, no, it's extremely serious. You see, 'Pataphysics has always existed. It's universal.

INTERVIEWER: Do pataphysicians, of which you are one, hold meetings?

IONESCO: From time to time, for promotions, decorations, commemorations, and pilgrimages. It's all very earnest.

INTERVIEWER: Just like the French Academy?

IONESCO: Much more. We have no uniforms, but we have insignia. For example, I am decorated with the *Ordre*

INTERVIEW CONTINUED ON PAGE 95

PLAY CONTINUED FROM PAGE 92

I'm going . . . For me every play is an adventure, a quest, the discovery of a universe that's suddenly revealed, and there's no one more surprised than I am to find that it exists . . .

BART I: We know all about that! Empirical stuff. You've explained it all before, dozens of times, in your previews, your articles and your interviews, about your creative mechanism, as you call it, though I don't like the word: "creative." "Mechanism" is all right though. I like that.

IONESCO: [*naïvely*] That's true, I *have* talked about my, sorry, creative mechanism before. You've a good memory!

BART I: Tell me more about your new play. What was it this time, the initial image that set off the process of construction . . .

IONESCO: Well . . . er. Well . . . er . . . It's rather complicated, you know . . . That's a really sticky question! . . . Oh well, here goes! The title of my new play is: The Shepherd's Chameleon.

BART I: Why The Shepherd's Chameleon?

IONESCO: It's the crucial scene of the play, the motive force. Once, in a large country town, in the middle of the street, during the summer, I saw a young shepherd, about three o'clock in the afternoon, who was embracing a chameleon . . . It was such a touching scene I decided to turn it into a tragic farce.

BART I: That's feasible scientifically.

IONESCO: It'll only be the starting-point. I don't know yet whether you'll really see the shepherd embracing the chameleon on the stage, or whether I'll simply call the scene to mind . . . Whether it'll just be an invisible background . . . drama once removed . . . In fact, I think it will only have to serve as a pretext . . .

BART I: Pity. The scene somehow seemed to me to illustrate the reconciliation of the Self with the Other.

IONESCO: You see, this time I'm going to put myself in the play!

BART I: That's all you ever do.

IONESCO: It won't be the last time, then.

BART I: Well, which are you to be, the shepherd or the chameleon?

IONESCO: Oh no, definitely not the chameleon. *I* don't change color every day . . . I'm not always being towed along by the latest fashion, like . . . but I'd rather not say who . . .

BART I: So you must be the shepherd then?

IONESCO: Not the shepherd either! I told you this was only a pretext, a starting point . . . In fact I put myself in the play to start off a discussion on the theater, to reveal my own ideas . . .

BART I: As you're not a scholar, you've no right to have ideas . . . That's where I come in.

IONESCO: Let's say my experiences, then . . .

BART I: Scientific experiment's the only experience that's valid.

IONESCO: . . . Well then . . . my beliefs . . .

BART I: Possible. But they're only provisional, we'll rectify them for you. Go on with your precarious exposition . . .

IONESCO: [*after a second's pause*] Thank you. You can say I *am* the shepherd if you like, and the theater's the chameleon. Because *I've* embraced a theatrical career, and the theater, of course, *changes*, for the theater is life. It's changeable like life . . . The chameleon's life too!

BART I: I note the formula, which is almost a thought.

IONESCO: So I'll talk about the theater . . . dramatic criticism and the public.

BART I: You need to be more of a sociologist for that!

IONESCO: . . . and the new drama, the essential character of which lies in its newness . . . I'll present my own points of view.

BART I: [*sweeping gesture*] Points of view with no optical instrument!

IONESCO: . . . It'll be an improvisation.

BART I: Read me what you've written so far, anyway.

IONESCO: [*pretending to hold back*] It's not quite ready. I told you . . . the dialogue's not tightened up. Still, I could read you a short extract.

BART I: I'm listening to you. I'm here to pass judgment on you. And put you right.

IONESCO: [*scratching his head*] I always find it rather embarrassing, you know, to read out what I've written. My own text makes me sick . . .

BART I: Autocriticism does honor to the writer, dishonor to the critic.

IONESCO: All right, I'll read it to you anyhow, so you won't have come for nothing. [BART I *settles himself down comfortably.*] This is how the play starts. "Scene One. Ionesco is asleep, his head on the table.

BRASSAI–RAPHO-GUILLUMETTE

Eugène Ionesco

PLAY CONTINUED ON PAGE 96

INTERVIEW CONTINUED FROM PAGE 93

de la Grande Gidouille [the Big Belly]. That's from Jarry's *Ubu Roi.* And I have the rank of Satrap. I'm very honored to belong to this group.

INTERVIEWER: Who are the great pataphysicians?

IONESCO: Raymond Queneau, Jacques Prévert, and Boris Vian before he died, were among them, but I believe that the actual rulers of 'Pataphysics are secret. Queneau, Dubuffet, René Clair, and myself—we're a front. We're there for glory. The real head of the Collège de 'Pataphysique is a gentleman by the name of Salmon who died recently and was reincarnated under the name of Latisane. I believe it's the same one.

INTERVIEWER: And who is Latisane?

IONESCO: It's Salmon.

INTERVIEWER: And this Latisane, what does he do in life?

IONESCO: He has a double who is a teacher. The Vice-Curator of the Collège de 'Pataphysique and the Perpetual President of the Supreme Council of Grand Masters of the *Ordre de la Grande Gidouille* is His Magnificence, Baron Jean Mollet.

INTERVIEWER: Who is Mollet?

IONESCO: He was the secretary of Guillaume Apollinaire the poet, author of *Calligrammes* and *Alcools*. His avocation is cooking.

INTERVIEWER: How was he elected to this position?

IONESCO: By unanimous vote, the only elector being Raymond Queneau. This is in the democratic tradition of the Collège de 'Pataphysique. Raymond Queneau wrote the name of Mollet on the ballot, cast the ballot in the urn, removed it himself, and thus the Baron was elected.

INTERVIEWER: Can 'Pataphysics be compared to any philosophy or body of thought?

IONESCO: In my opinion, 'Pataphysics is occidental Zen.

INTERVIEWER: How do you become a pataphysician?

IONESCO: One does not become a pataphysician, one *is* a pataphysician. For example, if you commit suicide, you are a pataphysician, and if you choose not to kill yourself, you are still a pataphysician. I was lecturing once to a group of foreign students, and at the end of the lecture one of them raised his hand and asked a very tricky question: "Are you a conscious or an unconscious pataphysician?"

INTERVIEWER: What would you answer to such a question?

IONESCO: I believe that the conscious pataphysicians are unconscious and the unconscious pataphysicians are conscious.

INTERVIEWER: What are some of the conscious or unconscious activities of a pataphysician?

IONESCO: The best activity is to refrain from all activity. That is why one of the greatest living pataphysicians is the Satrap Marcel Duchamp, the painter who anticipated Dadaism and who has been living in the United States. He now refrains from painting and devotes his life to playing chess.

INTERVIEWER: Does a pataphysician take vows?

IONESCO: Each one takes his own.

INTERVIEWER: And what vows have you taken as Satrap of the Collège de 'Pataphysique?

IONESCO: As Satrap I am for war and tyranny. I will exercise tyranny myself. As for war, I will have others wage it because I can't do two things at once.

INTERVIEWER: You have been influenced by the surrealists and the Dadaists, haven't you? In fact, the pataphysicians are, in a sense, Dadaists?

IONESCO: All of us came out of surrealism.

INTERVIEWER: What do you think of André Breton?

IONESCO: There are two men in France to whom you must listen without interruption. One is Cocteau, the most brilliant conversationalist I have encountered, and the other is André Breton—Cocteau because he is dazzling and Breton because he does not brook any interference, not even a question.

INTERVIEWER: Among your contemporaries, whom do you consider the best dramatist in France?

IONESCO: Samuel Beckett.

INTERVIEWER: Are you friends?

IONESCO: Yes. We see each other rarely, but we're good friends. Beckett is a fine fellow. He lives in the country with his wife, but we see each other when he comes in, at the theater, in cafés, in *brasseries*.

INTERVIEWER: Do you talk about the theater? What do you talk about?

IONESCO: We don't talk about anything much. He is a very generous man, very loyal. Those are rare qualities. I was told that for a long time his principal occupation was to play chess by himself.

INTERVIEWER: And Jean Genet, do you know him?

IONESCO: Oh, yes, we meet in literary salons.

INTERVIEWER: Does he still steal?

IONESCO: Possibly, just a little to keep up his reputation. You see, after a society woman has invited him, her friends call her to find out what is missing, and she is so happy if she can answer that it's an ash tray or a fork. So Genet obliges his hostess. He's a very decent sort of fellow.

INTERVIEWER: Is he rough in appearance and language?

IONESCO: Oh, no, he's *un homme de lettres*. In fact, he writes a little too well, don't you think? Like Giraudoux. That's his greatest fault.

INTERVIEWER: What other contemporary dramatists do you admire, outside of Beckett?

IONESCO: Friedrich Duerrenmatt and Boris Vian. Vian wrote a very interesting play, *Le Schwourtz,* a play which was badly received because it was very good, of course.

INTERVIEWER: It is obvious from your Molièresque impromptu, *The Shepherd's Chameleon,* that you do not think much of critics.

IONESCO: The trouble with most of them is that they want the artist to conform to some pre-established law of their invention.

INTERVIEWER: What is it that you mean when you speak of "anti-theater"?

IONESCO: The anti-theater is the theater. The so-called theatrical plays are

INTERVIEW CONTINUED ON PAGE 97

PLAY CONTINUED FROM PAGE 94

surrounded with books and manuscripts. A ball-point pencil is sticking out of one hand. A bell rings. Ionesco snores. Then there is the sound of beating on the door and cries of 'Ionesco! Ionesco!' Finally Ionesco jumps and rubs his eyes. Voice from outside the door: 'Ionesco! Are you there?' Ionesco: 'Yes . . . Just a second! . . . What's the matter now? . . .' Smoothing his untidy hair [*With these words* IONESCO *makes the gesture.*] Ionesco goes to the door and opens it; Bartholomeus appears. Bartholomeus: 'Glad I've found you in! I damned nearly went away, and I'd have been very angry, specially as you haven't a phone. What on earth were you doing?' Ionesco: 'I was working, working, I was writing! . . .' Bartholomeus: 'The new play? Is it ready? I'm waiting for it! . . .' Ionesco, sitting in his armchair and motioning Bartholomeus to a chair: 'Sit down!' "

[*While reading his play* IONESCO *sits down as before. At this moment the bell is really heard to ring, followed by a beating on the door.*]

ANOTHER MAN'S VOICE: Ionesco! Are you there?

[BART I, *who has been nodding his head in approbation during the reading, glances over to the door where the Voice comes from.*]

IONESCO: Yes, just a second. What's the matter now?

[*Smoothing his untidy hair,* IONESCO *goes to the door and opens it.* BARTHOLOMEUS II *appears.*]

BART II: Morning, Ionesco.

IONESCO: Morning, Bartholomeus.

BART II: [*to* BART I] Well, Bartholomeus, how are you?

BART I: [*to* BART II] Well, Bartholomeus, how are you?

BART II: Glad I've found you in! I damned nearly went away, and I'd have been very angry, specially as you haven't a phone . . . What on earth were you doing?

IONESCO: I was working, working, I was writing . . . Sit down!

[*He indicates a chair to* BART II *and sits down himself. There is more knocking on the door and a third man's voice:*]

THIRD MAN'S VOICE: Ionesco! Ionesco! Are you there?

IONESCO: Yes, just a second! What's the matter now?

[IONESCO *stands up, smooths his hair, makes for the door and opens it.* BARTHOLOMEUS III *appears, in a scholar's gown, like the others.*]

BART III: Morning, Ionesco.

IONESCO: Morning, Bartholomeus.

BART III: [*to* BART II] Well, Bartholomeus, how are you?

BART II: [*to* BART III] Well, Bartholomeus, how are you?

BART I: [*to* BART III] Well, Bartholomeus, how are you?

BART III: [*to* BART I] Well, Bartholomeus, how are you? [*To* IONESCO:] Glad I've found you in! I damned nearly went away, and I'd have been very angry, specially as you haven't a phone . . . What on earth were you doing?

[*The pace of the actors' delivery should increase.*]

IONESCO: I was working . . . working . . . I was writing!

BART III: The new play? Is it ready? I'm waiting for it.

IONESCO: [*sitting down and indicating a chair to* BART III] Sit down. [BART III *sits down by the others, all three in a row.*] Well, I'm working on it, you know. I've got right down to it. It's coming along, but it's not easy. It's got to be perfect, no repetition, no dull passages. I'm always being accused of going round in circles in my plays . . . so I'm tightening, tightening it up . . .

BART III: You can read us at least the beginning.

BART II: [*echo*] At least the beginning . . .

BART I: [*echo*] . . . least the beginning . . .

IONESCO: [*reading*] "Ionesco is asleep, his head on the table, surrounded with books and manuscripts. The doorbell rings. Ionesco snores. It rings again. Ionesco goes on snoring. Then there is a knocking at the door . . ."

[*Suddenly there is a real knocking at the door.*]

IONESCO: Yes, just a second! . . . What's the matter now?

[*Smoothing his untidy hair,* IONESCO *starts making for the door.*]

BART III: Sounds quite interesting . . . but let's hear the rest . . .

BART II: [*to* IONESCO] It's very unexpected.

[*Fresh knocking at the door.*]

BART I: [*to the other two*] That's because you weren't here from the start. I know this play a bit better. [*To* IONESCO:] It's a vicious circle. . . .

INTERVIEW CONTINUED FROM PAGE 95

anti-theatrical. They are false, full of tricks, too neat. The language is too literary, too beautiful. I am looking for something bare, something essential.

INTERVIEWER: Who are those dramatists who have influenced you?

IONESCO: Theatrical works have left almost no impression on me. I've read them in school, but I was completely detached from them. The works that have influenced me are works of philosophy and possibly some novels. There was a time when I liked Kafka very much; then at another time I liked Dostoevsky, Chekhov, Proust.

INTERVIEWER: Didn't you mention once that you wanted to write a play based on Proust's *Remembrance of Things Past*?

IONESCO: Yes. I'm in the process of rereading the whole thing now. I don't know what will remain. At times I am tempted by what is theatrical in Proust—the dinner at the house of Madame Verdurin, the reception at the Guermantes'. All this is fine theater. I am also tempted by what is less theatrical about the work. But in what terms does one work out a visualization of the passion of jealousy? It's very difficult.

INTEVIEWER: Since we're on the subject of Proust and your own interest in the novel, I would like to ask if you ever thought of writing one yourself.

IONESCO: Yes. I'm thinking of writing a novel which would be called *La Vase* [*Slime*]. It would be a novel of decomposition and reintegration. It would happen in a ditch. I would tell the story of a man who is in the process of decomposition and who is slowly sinking in the mud. He loses a leg, then an arm, then his whole body begins to decompose, until what remains is a vague contour in the mud, a form vaguely outlined in the slime.

INTERVIEWER: This ties in with your projected play about the dying king, doesn't it? Death is your leading preoccupation, or as you call it, obsession?

IONESCO: That's obvious.

INTERVIEWER: Do you recall when you first became conscious of death?

IONESCO: I was four years old, and I was with my mother in a room. We looked out the window, and there was a burial procession passing by. I asked my mother what it was, and she told me a man had died. Then I asked her how people came to die, and she said that it happened to them when they were old and sick. "And what does it mean to grow old?" I asked. "Does it mean that you hunch over more and more, and that you grow a white beard which gets longer and longer?" Yes, she said. "And does everyone grow old and die?" And she said yes again. Then I started to scream and to cry. I must have cried for hours.

INTERVIEWER: Were you religious as a child?

IONESCO: I wanted to be a saint. I went to church dutifully. Then one day a school chum offered me the first scientific refutation of the existence of God that I had heard. We were seven or eight at the time. My friend asked me where God was, and I told him that God was in heaven. "If God is in heaven," he said, "then how come we cannot see the bare soles of his feet right above us in the air?" To this day his argument seems to me to make as much sense as any of the longer philosophical discussions I have read on this side of the question.

INTERVIEWER: Do you believe in an after-life?

IONESCO: Who can tell? What I am certain of is that if it exists, it is bizarre.

INTERVIEWER: Death, destruction, and old age are your dominant themes, it seems.

IONESCO: Yes, but also beauty and sex. *Jack* is a highly erotic play, and so is *The Lesson*. Erotic possession is the hidden meaning of *The Lesson*. In *Jack* not much is hidden.

INTERVIEWER: *Jack* is the play about a bride with three noses. I am wondering what your idea of beauty is.

IONESCO: The bride in *Jack* has three faces rather than three noses. She was very beautiful in the Paris production. I think that when a type of beauty appears, it always seems ugly at first because it astonishes. Then it becomes beauty. Look at the actress Melina Mercouri in Jules Dassin's film *Never on Sunday*. She's probably the most beautiful woman in the world, and yet in a way she seems ugly. She's ugly and beautiful at once. Beauty is never pretty. It surprises first and then captivates and attaches.

INTERVIEWER: Could we end with a fundamental question: What do you consider the function of theater?

IONESCO: The only function of the theater, if we must speak of function, is to be theater, to *be*. Do we ask of a flower what function it serves? It simply exists, just as existence exists. The theater must teach people that there are activities which do not serve any purpose, which are gratuitous. Modern man does not understand that what is useful is more often than not a useless, crushing weight. Have you ever watched the inhabitants of a large city? They are harried creatures, prisoners of necessity. They run like dogs, their noses to the ground, along a well-traced course. They ought to walk like cats, aimlessly, slowly, gracefully. In our time people are terribly frightened of freedom and humor. They don't seem to realize that there is no life possible without these qualities. In that sense the theater is a supreme game: it is free action, and in it one must find a living language, not the language of realism but one that is based on the marvelous, fabled world, which has far greater reality than the so-called real world. The theater is the incarnation of dreams, of phantasmagoria. Bourgeois unrealism such as we find in the Broadway drama or the *théâtre des boulevards,* and socialistic unrealism as in the Brechtian plays, are the two greatest dangers which threaten the creative forces of the theater. A work of art is above all an adventure of the mind; it is the creation of an autonomous world introduced into our world from fundamental truths—which are those we find in dream and imagination.

Rosette Lamont, a writer and critic, is Assistant Professor of French and Comparative Literature at Queens College.

On Stage: ANNE MEACHAM

Twenty years or so ago, as a junior at New Trier High School in Winnetka, a suburb of Chicago, Anne Meacham was cast as the heroine of *Death Takes a Holiday* and immediately after the performance—her first before an audience—was accorded an extraordinary clairvoyance. "For the first time in my life," she recalled not long ago, "I felt completely safe. I didn't have to speak *my* words—which I didn't consider adequate. I didn't have to handle a situation—the playwright had created it. He had given me my personality—what was needed of me and would be acceptable. I had an area of safety that I had nowhere else in my life."

The insight was bleak and perfect. Four years later Miss Meacham, having left the University of Rochester (she had decided that her voice was too small to carry her through the Eastman School of Music and into opera), became a student at the Yale School of Drama at the same time as Julie Harris. "One day I walked into the Green Room—the library, actually," she said, "and she was seated at a table—rust hair, I remember, a rust-colored sweater, a pile of books on either side of her face. She looked up between them and I looked at her. *Neither of us said a word.* But she knew she could act, and, I felt, she knew that I wasn't sure I was an actress. I was terrified at my awareness and I left." Since then, both on and off Broadway, Miss Meacham has been given reason to be certain that not merely is she an actress but one of a very wide range. For she has been seen in roles as disparate as Ibsen's Hedda Gabler; as Lizzie Borden, the murderous spinster of Fall River; as the tormented Catherine whose sanity a possessive mother attempted to destroy in Tennessee Williams's *Suddenly Last Summer;* as the luminous Aurora in *The Immortal Husband;* and as Ensign Jane Hilton in *The Long Watch,* in which she made her Broadway debut in 1952 and won a Clarence Derwent Award for the best performance by a nonfeatured actress.

Actors change their names, train their voices, improve their diction and carriage, and curry their bodies; but Miss Meacham, in the pursuit of safety, or the illusion of it, has clearly been extravagant. She was born, as she put it with characteristic precision, "at three o'clock in the afternoon of July 21, 1922, in the Lying-In Hospital in Chicago and named Mary Anne Meacham." At various times she called herself Sydney Foster, Anne Gaylord, and Christine Lord, discarding the last upon receipt of a letter from her father, addressed sardonically to "Dear J. C." She spent two years using her already trained mezzo-soprano to expunge her flat Midwest inflections (though she can reproduce them as an actress), replacing them with a flawless, international stage English. In fine, she has fashioned herself into an actress of high accomplishment and is regarded as an ornament of the American theater by discriminating playgoers.

Miss Meacham is above middle height and slender; her eyes are an equivocal gray-blue; her features are delicate and beautiful, almost marmoreal in their flawlessness, conveying the odd effect of an ageless piece of Meissen animated by what a producer has spoken of as her "quick, quick intelligence." She is, in fact, an actress in the classical manner, the finest of instruments for the playwright who will, as she says, "state the areas of personality for me so that I know which aspect of myself to give" and thus armor her. Hence, last winter she was able to create in less than seventy-two hours (she slept fewer than eight) a Hedda Gabler of a quality that, by general critical agreement, had not been seen in New York for decades: a creature so full of ignoble longing and divine rage, of pity and terror, of ruthlessness and remorse, as to exhaust the audiences that came nightly to see her and yet somehow not to dwarf the cast with which she was playing.

"I don't think a normal person could have done it," says David Ross, the formidable producer-director of off-Broadway's Fourth Street Theater, who will send his successful *Hedda Gabler* on tour this fall. "It was a question of life or death. I don't know what her reasons for life or death were, but I knew mine—my entire production was at stake." On the Saturday night preceding the Tuesday of the first preview, Mai Zetterling, the Swedish star whom Ross had imported to play the role, collapsed. At 2:15 A.M. Sunday, Ross managed to reach Miss Meacham by telephone at her Greenwich Village apartment. By Tuesday she had mastered the four-act play and before an audience that evening produced her Hedda Gabler. "She did what most actresses today fail to do," Ross says. "She *got* the author—she so submerged herself that she was Hedda Gabler, not a personality. She is—I can think of no higher compliment—a repertory actress."

"I belong in the theater," Miss Meacham says, "because I have been moved and released and touched and understood in it. My own sense of aliveness has been heightened by other people. The most excruciating knowledge of pain I had ever experienced, I felt in watching Laurence Olivier's Oedipus. When I saw Laurette Taylor in *The Glass Menagerie,* my whole being was shaken. I don't know if it's reward enough, but I won't do anything else but act." She spread her hands on the table behind which she was sitting. "No," she said, "I won't."

GILBERT MILLSTEIN

Photograph by HANS NAMUTH

On Stage: MILES DAVIS

When Miles Davis—a small, taut, princely man of thirty-four who is possibly the most gifted trumpet player to be heard since the apotheosis of Louis Armstrong—concluded his first engagement in London last fall, the jazz critic of the *Daily Mail* wrote of him, "This sour and surly sorehead is a genius." The persimmony tone of the judgment describes accurately the manner in which Davis abrades the sensibilities and enthralls the senses of his auditors, to say nothing of his employers, who are almost invariably enriched, if not warmed, by his presence. They pay the Miles Davis Quintet anywhere from $2,500 for a single concert to $4,000 or more a week for night-club appearances, and, practical men all, suffer its leader's intransigencies as they would the weather.

Davis is governed by a logic of internal economy so reasonable and orderly as to make him seem an alien in a world he considers to be both unreasonable and disorderly. Everything he does is intended to serve the ends of his music. When he is working he will neither announce what he intends to play nor acknowledge requests or applause; sometimes, while his colleagues are playing, he will leave the stand to commune darkly in a corner with whatever private gods he recognizes. "My attitude is, I play good music and that's it," he says. "If I'm not drunk they get what they're coming to hear, but I've got nothing to do with what they've come to *see*. If you start acting the way people think you are or should be, you're screwed up." A friend of Davis's states the case this way: "Miles plays, you applaud, and it's a draw. Why should he bow and make it two to one?"

This refusal to compromise is part of an aggressively personal pursuit of his calling that places Davis, along with Thelonius Monk and Ornette Coleman, among the most romantic of modern jazz instrumentalists. His style, or what the profession calls his "conception," is easily identifiable: in keeping with his philosophy, it is free from encumbrance—lean, reticent, its lyrical peaks offset by quiet plateaus of controlled, assured playing and by valleys of deep introspection. The sound of the Davis trumpet—characteristically, it is often muted—is extraordinarily pure, being almost without vibrato or crescendo and diminuendo. Often, in its delicate statement of a ballad or subtle development of a modern-jazz motif, one hears the modes and rhythms of the East.

Davis grew up in East St. Louis, Illinois, where his father was a dentist, and began playing the trumpet at the age of thirteen at the suggestion of one of his father's patients. When the Billy Eckstine band came to town several years later, young Miles sat in for two weeks alongside his idols Dizzy Gillespie and Charlie Parker, and in 1945, resisting his mother's efforts to send him to Fisk University, he came to New York to seek out Parker. Though he was enrolled in the Juilliard School of Music, Davis did most of his listening and learning at the jazz clubs on Fifty-second Street, and, with encouragement from Parker and others, he developed into an outstanding young "bop" trumpeter. In 1948 he assembled a nine-piece recording group that was important in establishing the "cool" jazz prevalent during the fifties; its arrangers were Gerry Mulligan, John Lewis, and Gil Evans, who has continued to write extensively for the various ensembles Davis has led during his rise to eminence.

This success has altered the surface of Davis's life (he now drives a $12,000 Ferrari, wears custom-tailored suits, and buys abstract paintings for his remodeled brownstone on Manhattan's West Side), but has not affected its inner quality of almost combative integrity. It is apt that one of Davis's few preoccupations outside of music is boxing. He generally goes several times a week to a fighter's gymnasium, and he is wont to make analogies based on the sport. "Archie Moore fought Harold Johnson fourteen rounds," he recalls, "and Johnson was clobbering him with that left. Then Archie tells him in a clinch, 'Boy, that left is killing me.' After that the left got pretentious, and Archie knocked him out in the fifteenth—Johnson got self-conscious and started acting the way the old man wanted him to. He became a puppet."

Davis knows how it feels to be a puppet, for he was a narcotics addict for four years. He broke the habit with inexorable reason: drugs left him powerless to play the way he wanted. To Davis, music is "a disease—a divine disease." Lying on a bed in his home not long ago, an arm over his eyes against the light, he remarked that he feels weak and irritable until he gets on the stand to perform. "Music is like having a habit," he said. "Only this one you can't break. You never feel like other people." He raised himself on an elbow and rolled over. "I know one of these days I'm going to walk off the stand and never play again. Something's going to touch me. And when that happens, I'll divorce myself from the trumpet." He thought about the prospect for a moment. "But not music, not the disease," he conceded with a faint smile. "I could spend the rest of my life listening, day and night, and be busy." GILBERT MILLSTEIN

Photograph by MARTIN DAIN

CAMELOT: *though two wizard*

A sketch for Camelot *by designer Oliver Smith*

"When they praise the sets and costumes," says a theatrical adage, "you're in trouble." What it means, of course, is that the critics found nothing else in the show to praise, and over the years Broadway has applied it to any number of fancy-dressed turkeys that dazzled the eye and dazed the mind.

Probably no sets and costumes have ever been praised more highly than the ones shown on these pages, which are from *Camelot*, the Arthurian musical by Alan Jay Lerner and Frederick Loewe. Nor, perhaps, has a show ever been in such famous trouble or disappointed so many people with its flaws. True to the adage, the critics celebrated *Camelot's* looks and then soon ran out of compliments.

This does not mean, however, that it will languish at the box office and silently steal away. On the contrary, it will play to full houses for several years and remain a conversation piece. Its songs will saturate the nation, and so will various commercial products derived from the show. *Camelot* will also travel across America, run many a foggy day in London town, and eventually turn up in a resplendent version on the screen. It will, in short, be around for quite a while.

Behind this paradox—the long life of the show versus the short shrift by the critics—there obviously lie certain elements of magic, as potent as any that Merlyn himself could conjure up. The magic words are "Lerner and Loewe." Writing *My Fair Lady* has put them outside the mortal laws of the theater. They do not bring to Broadway so much a show as an institution. As every woman knows, their preceding show shaped the fashions of an entire season. It also sired "My Fair Lady" dolls, watches, coloring books, tea sets, towels, jewelry, fabrics, and various other artifacts, as well as a "My Fair Lady Rose."

Camelot is making a comparable dent on the national scene. A "Camelot Rose" is now being bred. Louis Marx, the biggest toymaker in the land, will issue a model village of Camelot; the show's costumes have inspired bright tunics and other "Arthurian" styles; a hoop-throwing game similar to the one that diverts Queen Guenevere at her Maying party has appeared on the market; and the boys' world of toy soldiers is swelling with miniature Knights of the Round Table.

But the biggest proof of Lerner and Loewe's position in

By WILLIAM K. ZINSSER

rought it to Broadway, the magic of it lies all in visual splendor

the mythology of the modern theater is that they move the public to astonishing acts of faith. *Camelot* took its first advertisement more than eight months before its New York opening on December 3, 1960. The ad, which announced in the New York *Times* of March 27 the reuniting of the *My Fair Lady* team of Lerner, Loewe, director Moss Hart, and star Julie Andrews, drew 40,000 mail-order replies, and eventually the advance sale grew to more than $2,000,000.

Just as bewitching a tune was played by the two pied pipers in the case of the original-cast record album. Before *Camelot* reached Broadway, before the record was even made, more than 250,000 copies were bought and paid for. Everybody who was anybody—and millions who weren't—awaited the première, which promised to be the most lustrous event of the theatrical season.

Such a huge fund of money and esteem, while financially soothing, turned out to be a harsh abrasive in almost every other respect. Lerner and Loewe quickly found themselves the victims of their own corporate image. For when *Camelot* was finally unveiled last fall in Toronto, reporters flocked from all over the continent to let their readers know if the show was as good as its radiant older sister, *My Fair Lady*.

"It was like taking a small Balkan war on tour," says Richard Maney, *Camelot*'s press agent. For all was not well with *Camelot*. First, the opening-night curtain in Toronto did not descend until 12:30 A.M. All musicals run long at their out-of-town premières, but not *that* long; clearly a drastic pruning job lay ahead. At this point, however, Lerner was hospitalized with bleeding ulcers, and *Camelot* postponed its New York debut by two weeks. Then Moss Hart had a coronary attack that put him out of action. As Loewe already had a bad heart and the show's original costumer, Adrian, had died in mid-assignment, an aura of doom settled over the production that had once looked so golden.

Lerner rose from his sickbed to replace Hart as director. This hardly proved good therapy for an ulcer patient, for Lerner found that he not only had to cut the show extensively but rewrite much of it, redirect it accordingly, and add new songs to splice the severed ends together. Thus he imposed on himself a task so heavy that he worked twenty hours a day until *Camelot* limped to Broadway six weeks later.

During this period the New York papers carried frequent items about the surgery the musical was undergoing. These gloomy reports evoked little sympathy; as a matter of fact, they acted as an autumn tonic on the habitués of Sardi's and Shubert Alley. For to the practitioners of the stage nothing is so exhilarating as to see the gods tumble from Olympus. Some years ago an eminent playwright and wit was told the joyful news that a play produced by Richard Rodgers and Oscar Hammerstein 2nd had folded in Boston; he listened gravely and said: "You've got me all wrong. I *like* Dick and Oscar. I want them to have a hit, I really do . . . not as much as I want them to have a *flop*, of course." This sentiment echoed again through the salons of Manhattan as *Camelot* approached on feet of clay. "I hear it *still* runs forty minutes long," a rival producer would only have to say to an unemployed actor to put them both in high spirits, and the wags soon had a favorite epithet for the show: "It's *Parsifal* without the laughs."

As of last fall, therefore, Lerner and Loewe were suffering both the natural shocks that flesh is heir to and the proud man's contumely. The latter they had partly brought upon themselves by their institutional mien. During the summer and autumn, for instance, they turned up in various magazines in portraits by Karsh of Ottawa. Short of being carved into Mount Rushmore, there are few surer ways of looking important than to be photographed by Karsh, and the two men posed over a piano in such solemnity that they would seem to have written nothing less than *Tristan und Isolde*.

In view of the build-up (and the $650,000 gross cost of the show, $480,000 of which was put up by the Columbia Broadcasting System), Lerner and Loewe must have found their final ordeal with *Camelot* a bitter climax to two years of hard work. For they are sincere artists, and the show's faults are largely faults of sincerity. Nor is it all that faulty. If not a bird of paradise, it is no turkey, and this in itself was a feat, considering the task that the authors had set out to do.

Lerner and Loewe, whose collaboration goes back eighteen years and also includes *Brigadoon* and *Paint Your Wagon*, were stuck for a project when, in 1958, T. H. White's novel *The Once and Future King*, a retelling of the Arthurian legend, was published in America. In August an associate drew

Lerner's attention to White's book and its theatrical possibilities. "I fell in love with the man immediately," says Lerner, a small and scholarly man of forty-two with an angular face and serious eyes, who talks with a lyricist's easy precision. "Not with the age of chivalry per se, but with King Arthur himself. I also read Malory's *Morte d'Arthur* and William Morris's *Defence of Guenevere,* but actually I didn't do much research. I did enough to realize that the legend was pure fiction, and that gave me the liberty to create my own legend.

"Still, it obviously had a germ of truth. I suddenly understood why the legend has persisted: the concept of the Round Table, where men of different factions sit in peace, is the universal dream. You find in the Welsh version, which dates from the seventh century, that Arthur does not die but is taken to a cave, where he and his knights are waiting to be called back to the Round Table. In all versions of the legend the hope is expressed that Arthur will return.

"T. H. White's book traces the journey of an innocent man in a barbarous world, who tries to establish chivalry and justice, sees his dream dismembered, but finds hope at the end that his plan will survive, at least as an idea."

"I followed that arc," Lerner says, "though I didn't follow White's book closely." He did, however, extract its central concept, which reminded him of Learned Hand's speech "The Spirit of Liberty," especially the paraphrase of H. G. Wells about "Him who, near two thousand years ago, taught mankind that lesson it has never learned, but has never quite forgotten." To Lerner "that's the core of King Arthur."

"The other thing that fascinated me," says Lerner, "was why Arthur allowed the illicit love affair between Guenevere and Lancelot to flourish under his roof. This part of the legend was born much later—in eleventh-century France—but still it is never explained. In *Camelot,* I try to explain it with the soliloquy that ends Act I."

In this speech Arthur declares that the affair has wounded him and that he craves a man's vengeance. But he goes on to say that he is not a man but a king, a king trying to set civilized standards, and he will not destroy the things he loves. "This is the time of King Arthur," he cries, "and violence is not strength, and compassion is not weakness."

It is no ordinary librettist who would build a Broadway musical around such an earnest theme or end his first act on such a cerebral point. But Lerner has never let convention be his guide. "If you start on a project because you think, 'This has all the ingredients of a good musical,' you're doomed," he says. "The first requisite is to fall in love with your material. In this case the material dictated a classical form, with soliloquies and that sort of thing."

Equally basic is the problem of setting a musical mood for the show. Lerner's partner Frederick Loewe never goes at this task academically. "I'm not a research man—I'm too lazy," he says, "but I do have a solid musical background." This is a fair statement for a man who was a piano prodigy at five, played with the Berlin Philharmonic at twelve, and is versed in the operatic traditions of his native Vienna.

Now fifty-nine, Loewe is the antithesis of his young partner. Where Lerner is frail and nimble, meticulous in speech and unemotional in manner, Loewe is heavy and bearish; his German-accented words spill out in unruly clusters, and he has an outward warmth, as befits his reputation as *boulevardier* and man-about-continents. But unlike that other disparate team, Gilbert and Sullivan, the two men enjoy working together and do so in perfect concord.

"I don't try to make my music authentic," Loewe says. "I have to feel a style, dream it up. It's not authenticity that counts—it's effect. *Brigadoon* got smash notices in Edinburgh, but the music isn't Scottish. Real Scottish tunes sound like Hebrew laments, and if I had used anything like that, I would have driven the audience out. Instead I had to evolve a style that was gay and would not lose its pulse. I have a tendency to write folk songs. 'Come to Me, Bend to Me,' from *Brigadoon,* is considered a folk song in Scotland now."

"I get terribly upset," Loewe says, "when people call me a song writer. I'm a dramatic composer. That's a business in itself—to feel a mood. In *Gigi,* for instance, I tried to write

TEXT CONTINUED ON PAGE 113

The Pomp of CAMELOT

One man made famous by Lerner and Loewe's musical play on the Arthurian legend is costume designer Tony Duquette, a portfolio of whose original models and drawings for the most glamorously accoutred production of our times appears on the following eight pages. Taking up as his first Broadway assignment the work commenced by the famed Hollywood designer Adrian upon the latter's untimely death, Duquette—while retaining some of Adrian's designs and adapting many others —created most of Camelot's *wardrobe himself. Altogether some four hundred and fifty individual costumes were designed for the show; three hundred adorn it today, some of Duquette's finest, such as those for the Sirens (pages 110–111), Arthur (page 107), and the Black Knight (page 112), having been discarded as the scenes for which he devised them were sheared off during the tryouts.*

Duquette employed a variety of techniques to demonstrate to the show's producers and to his own workshop the precise effects he sought: thus we have two-foot-high maquettes of great refinement to suggest the members of Morgan Le Fey's band (two of which are shown opposite); a drawing incorporating swatches of fabric in the equestrian figure for the joust (pages 106–107—Duquette customarily finds his fabrics, then designs); and lush gouaches to convey a sense of enchantment for the dream ballet in Morgan Le Fey's forest (pages 108–109). In the end it was apparent that Duquette had worked his own enchantment, in which his and Adrian's artistry (as in the latter's costume for Guenevere, page 107) were fused into a magnificent whole.

Arthur

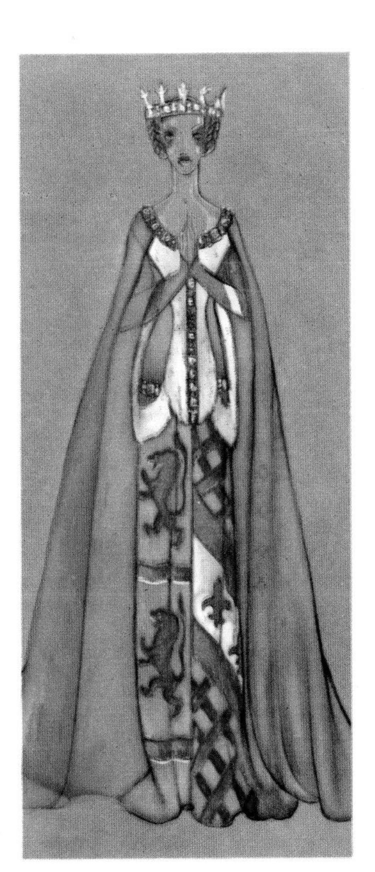

Guenevere

Duquette
167

TEXT CONTINUED FROM PAGE 104

a score that gives you that Parisian flavor without being antique." Loewe strode to the piano to illustrate the point, as he frequently does, in this case with "The Night They Invented Champagne." At these moments there is a spring in his step, a smile in his grayish-blue eyes, and a lilt of Vienna in his playing, as if inwardly he heard a full string orchestra accompanying him. The playing style, like the man and his music, is clearly a product of Europe. There is none of the brittleness, the uniquely American sophistication—or the originality—of George Gershwin and Richard Rodgers. In his romantic airs and pure harmonies, Loewe remains a man of the Danube far more than of the Hudson.

Finding a mood for *Camelot* wasn't easy. "After all," Loewe says, "it's set four or five hundred years before music existed, that we know of. Therefore it shouldn't be operatic or symphonic. Actually, *Camelot* consists of many musical styles. It starts as romantic comedy, goes on to drama, returns to romance, and ends in tragedy."

While Lerner and Loewe were constructing their Camelot in words and music, designer Oliver Smith began doing research for the sets. "Rather than taking a straight historical approach," Smith says, "we jumped all over, at least four or five hundred years. We wanted to create a complete fantasy world of our own. I was influenced by the Book of Hours of the Duc de Berry and also by French illuminated manuscripts and early French painters, especially Fouquet. Paradoxically, there's almost no English influence in the sets. But then the Arthurian legend is one that we don't take literally anyhow, especially in America. It's treated more in the realms of literature and the imagination."

Smith took a year's trip before starting on *Camelot*, mostly to Mediterranean lands, and looked at paintings and everything else with the show in mind. "You try to absorb that entire visual world in a brief period," he says. "It's a very interesting experience. I even got to the point where I was seeing contemporary landscapes in medieval terms. Incidentally, they look a good deal better that way. I was also strongly affected by Hieronymus Bosch and other Flemish painters whose work I saw in the Prado. The Bosch influence may not seem noticeable in the sets, but it's there as a base. I also made a trip to St. Catherine's Monastery in the Sinai Peninsula, which has the biggest collection of medieval icons in the world. They're very Byzantine—mainly gold leaf on wood. They had a direct bearing on my design for the Great Hall and for the small living room. But when I got down to work I put all my research aside and didn't look at it again."

The task of clothing *Camelot* also involved research, imaginative leaps and bounds, and trouble of its own. Adrian made his first sketches before the script was written or the sets designed, but then he died. Tony Duquette was engaged to carry on—an assignment that had its thorns as well as its roses. On the one hand it was a chance to design the most sumptuous clothes ever to adorn a musical, representing an age of fable which most people find unbearably romantic. On the other hand he had to continue harmoniously another man's work and to realize that nobody would know where Adrian's inspiration had left off and his own had begun.

"Adrian's sketches consisted mostly of Guenevere's dresses," Duquette explains. "I did most of the men's costumes and also established the palette of the production. I didn't make any attempt to be literal. This is supposed to be a brilliant fantasy to capture the mood of a fairy story. Of course I did a good deal of research in the Book of Hours and in Viollet-le-Duc. Also, the costumes in the joust scene reflect the influence of the old tarot playing cards, especially in their vivid colors. But on the whole it's a fantastic approach to armor and everything else. Even the heraldry is incorrect. The show will probably drive the experts mad—Arthurian-legend people are just violent, you know."

Thus handsomely endowed, *Camelot* reached Broadway three harrowing months after it had gone into rehearsal. An extraordinarily glittering crowd turned out to inspect it, and they found much to please them: a sumptuous production, a luminous Guenevere in Julie Andrews, a regal Arthur in Richard Burton; Loewe's score was melodious, and often stately; and Lerner's lyrics, if rarely brilliant, were always craftsmanlike in their clean lines. Gay and humorous in its first half-hour, *Camelot* seemed a sure champion. Then a strange disunity set in, and the show veered among many incongruous moods. It became, successively, an ironic tale of knighthood, a pageant, a romantic triangle, a somber monodrama, a fantasy, a plea for peace and brotherhood, a Shubert operetta, and finally a tragedy. Attempting to make too many points, it made none well, lost momentum, and dragged laboriously to its end. Only Richard Burton's performance as King Arthur, shining through the disorder, gave the play coherence.

These faults were cited in detail by the critics, nearly all of whom pointed out that *Camelot* was no *My Fair Lady*. Perhaps it could have been if it had maintained the light spirit of the first half-hour. Yet Lerner and Loewe had aimed at something more serious; and if they fell short of the mark, it was still a high mark to aim for.

Probably the most valid point was made by Hobe Morrison, the critic for *Variety*. He wondered "what the response would have been if *Camelot* had been written by unknowns." Almost certainly it would have been welcomed with gratitude, regardless of its flaws. For it is a show that commands respect in an age of musicals that seek cheap solutions. It does not bring on the girls; it does not end happily; it gives the audience an idea to ponder. And its sets and costumes, of course, are stunning.

My Fair Lady will remain the once and future queen of musicals, but *Camelot* is at least a cousin of the queen, and no poor cousin either.

William K. Zinsser is a free-lance writer whose comments on the lively arts have appeared frequently in HORIZON.

MOVIES

Samurai, With Sword, Won't Travel

If a certain amount of confusion arises in the minds of movie-goers concerning *The Magnificent Seven,* it may be understandable. For the current Western is an adaptation to south-of-the-border tradition of the laurel-crowned Japanese film *Seven Samurai,* which itself had been titled *The Magnificent Seven* for its release in the United States in 1956. At that time it was saluted by the critics as a splendid "Japanese Western." It was nothing of the sort, but the misunderstanding may have encouraged Yul Brynner and others to purchase the rights for a remake. The new product deserves a well-intentioned if modest trophy as a straightforward Western diversion.

Eli Wallach, as the leader of forty bad men whose victims are hard-working and indigent peasants, turns in a lusty performance, never overexposing the conspicuous gold tooth in the front of his head but allowing it to glint strategically from time to time like a personal badge of wickedness; Yul Brynner, overwashed, his haberdashery immaculate at all times, is the standard-bearer for the seven gunhands who rescue the beleaguered underdogs, and occasionally he is a little better than fair to middling; two of his lieutenants, Steve McQueen (laconic, cool as a cucumber) and Horst Buchholz (ebullient, headlong) make up, in extremes of temperature, for his tepidity. The scenes—the farmers' melancholy village, the dusty hills of Mexico with niggardly growth of mesquite, a barbarous jerkwater border town populated by louts and brutes—are photographed well in honest color. The gait proceeds from walk to trot to canter to gallop; the fighting is declamatory, the deaths are abundant and excruciating, the men and horses are in the pink of condition. On the whole, the two hours of the picture are energetic and entertaining.

However, if one considers this Occidental product in the light of its Oriental predecessor in black and white, one wonders how John Sturges, the producer and director, had the nerve to steal the thunder of his counterpart, Akira Kurosawa. A comparison of the Japanese and the American versions shows certain ingenious fidelities in Mr. Sturges's adaptation; his elisions are wise; the liberties he takes in altering or reassigning the rationales of individual men are discreet and pardonable though not always understandable; the narrative itself (and a cinematic humdinger it is) is not greatly changed; the message has been renovated to suit a contemporary Western audience. But the essence, peculiar to the original, has evaporated; by the time the 1450 *sake* has got to Chihuahua, it has lost its bouquet and acquired the taste of 1880 five-cent whiskey. The experience is rather like seeing an adaptation of a story from *Le Morte d'Arthur* with the search for the Holy Grail transferred to the Texas Panhandle.

In both pictures the ruffians, while differently accoutered (helmets adorned with crescents, and bows and arrows for the Japanese, sombreros and six-shooters for the Mexicans), are birds of a feather, annually descending with a whoop and a holler on the unprotected settlements after the harvest to pillage the grain and rape the women. And the peasants in both are timeless and universal innocents, unacquainted with worldly violence and voracity, superstitious, xenophobic, forever fearful of the caprices of nature, the rotting rains, the desiccating droughts, the winds that derange the fields, the pestilences of blight and bugs. To be at the mercy of freebooters as well makes their lot intolerable. In both villages there is a venerable sage, known simply as "the old man," who chides his wretched neighbors for their timidity and counsels them to take a stand against their persecutors. But the men are baffled; they protest that they have no weapons for defense and, even if they had, they would not know how to fight. Then, say the respective ancients, they must *get* weapons and hire experts to train them. Finally, still skeptical, the desperate farmers are persuaded, and delegations set forth to buy arms and recruit teachers.

Now East and West diverge, for while both heptads of trouble shooters are soldiers of fortune, the Japanese are professional military men as well, pledged to the hereditary ethic of the samurai to live by courage and in stoicism, to despise money, never to disgrace their swords, the wearing of which is the highest honor they can conceive. These swords must not be drawn for frivolous reasons but, if the provocation is justifiable, they must then not be returned to their scabbards until they have accomplished their mission of mercy or the avenging of honor. Thus, the seven Japanese who undertake to annihilate the forty thieves are affiliated by caste. In answering the peasants' appeal, they are adhering to a chivalric code from which, as individuals, they may have deviated but to which, when the summons comes, they return without hesitation. This return to an ideal is something every Japanese spectator recognizes, just as a Scot would recognize a resumption of the moral obligations of a Highland clan. The rules and rituals of the samurai estate are woven into the tale to produce a dense, stylized operatic texture, often grotesque but seldom interfering with the development of the action, and the action, founded on fact and tradition, is entirely credible.

Lacking in this historic dimension, the westerners of Sturges's epic are united in a loose camaraderie that derives from their common talent with guns, their rootlessness, their appetite for dangerous adventure. But while the pistol-packing Good Samaritan, champion of widows and orphans, is now a traditional figure, he is wanting in the impressive authority of organized knight-errantry. It seems quite improbable that seven paragons should emerge from the scum of one small frontier region.

In both cases the leader of the group is approached by the farmers after a demonstration of selfless heroism; the samurai rescues a child who is being held hostage by a thief; Yul Brynner, assisted by Steve McQueen, buries an Indian in a white cemetery in defiance of tumultuous racism. And to each group a maverick attaches himself; they are both peasants by birth but deny their origin, damn the farmers as liars and swindlers, hope that the glory of their virile confederates will rub off on them but, in combat, reveal themselves for what they are in their fierce defense of their own people. Kurosawa's yokel claims to be a samurai, and he carries a stolen sword a good foot longer than convenient for him; he has, as well, papers purloined from a corpse whose vital statistics could not possibly correspond with his own. Rebuffed, told to leave the work of the samurai to the samurai, this man, with the stature of a Brobdingnagian and the visage of a Yahoo, refuses to take No for an answer and tags along as the authentic warriors make their way to the village. He drinks himself into a feral condition; he growls and howls and roars; he whimpers, keens like a banshee, giggles like a witch adding prime specimens of newts' eyes to her brew, whirls like a dervish, hops, skips, grimaces. He will not be shaken off, and eventually, although they scorn him, the samurai must accept him. In the final battle he rescues an orphaned infant from a burning mill, and rocking the child in his arms, sobs that the same thing happened to him when he was a baby. Mortally wounded, he kills the chief of the bandits and dies nobly in triumph. He is the traditional clown, outlandish, simian, chuckleheaded, and ultimately admirable—an arbitrary character, perhaps, but an acceptable one.

Sturges's farm boy, excellently played by Horst Buchholz, proves his mettle, but unlike the buffoon he paraphrases, he survives, and falling in love with one of the village girls, he relinquishes his dreams of being an itinerant fast gun, accepts his inexorable destiny, and resuming his birthright, settles for a bucolic life. In the Japanese version, it is one of the samurai, a very young man, who falls in love with a beautiful young girl from the village. He yearns to remain with her, but at the end—with her complete understanding, one feels—recognizes the stronger bond of obligation to his caste and its stoic code and departs toward the solitary, severe life of his colleagues and idols.

In both movies the preparations of the good men for the arrival of the villains are painstaking and extensive. They build fortifications, draw up maps of the probable approaches of the raiders, establish sentries, teach the clumsy farmers how to kill. By the time the crops are in, the trap is set. The showdown, when it finally comes, is fulminating; but the gunplay of the Western melee is not a patch on the swordplay of the Eastern, with its splendid show of agility and muscular verve. All forty of the rascals are done in, and all but three of the Boy Scouts; and the villagers rejoice amongst the cadavers. In Kurosawa's original, the remaining samurai, their work done, are shown leaving to do new deeds of valor; order has been restored, the dead have been buried, and planting time is here again. When they have gained a rise of land the three pause and look back upon a peaceful scene of women working in the rice and millet fields as the men make music; everyone bends and sways like graceful grain in the wind. "Again we have survived," the old samurai says, "but again we have lost." The winners of peace are the caretakers of the land, not the warriors.

Similarly as Yul Brynner and Steve McQueen ride off, they turn back to watch Horst Buchholz run to join his sweetheart, who is grinding corn. They regret that they can never be domesticated. But in the original, that is not the point at all. The samurai do not regret that they are samurai, and they would despise a cottage small by a waterfall. What they do regret—or what is foreshadowed in Kurosawa's film—is that their proud class is doomed and that the honors accruing to their station will soon be merely symbolic.

—JEAN STAFFORD

BOOKS

Our Man in Purgatory

In his latest novel, *A Burnt-Out Case,* Graham Greene returns to the region where he feels most at home: a seedy outpost of the Western world, in which religion and altruism attack disease, barbarism, stupidity, and evil, with the odds (at least in human terms) against the attackers. The scene is a leper colony in West Africa. It reminds us of Dr. Schweitzer's Lambaréné or of the hospital in *The Nun's Story,* except that both those institutions take in many different kinds of sick people, whereas this one concentrates on the most dreadful and repulsive. Nowadays it is possible to cure leprosy and to treat even quite advanced cases so that they degenerate no further. Sometimes the resistance of the patient combined with the treatment seems to exhaust the power of the disease, so that, having done almost all the harm it can, it withdraws, leaving the body mutilated and deformed. A patient who has suffered this trial will never have leprosy again, but he will never be fully human again either. Crippled, hideous, benumbed, he is a burnt-out case.

Sin is for the soul what leprosy is for the body, and spreads like it: first a patch, the size of a coin, on some noticeable place such as the hand or the cheek; then a thickening of the skin; then a change of the face and an alteration of the voice; then a transformation into something as nearly animal as human. The hero of Greene's book has had spiritual leprosy. He was once successful (as a modern architect), and rich, and selfish, and a great lover of women. Now he is totally exhausted and somehow deafened and deadened, as though his spiritual tissues had been through some harsh and final transformation. He has given up his career, left Europe and America behind, and come, as though in flight, to the most wretched place in the saddest continent on our planet. A thousand, even five hundred years ago he would have become a monk. But now he cannot. He is unable to believe in God; or else he cannot believe that God sends grace to repentant sinners, that Jesus died to redeem them, and that he is one of those who can be saved. He can only suffer numbly, with a perpetual consciousness of being spiritually corroded and distorted. Like the crippled servant who is assigned to look after him when he arrives, he is a burnt-out case.

What happens to him in the leper colony scarcely matters. It does not matter at all to him; for although he lives and moves and talks, he is spiritually all but dead. He builds a hospital for the priests and nuns and doctors who care for the lepers; he does an act of self-sacrifice, with little more effort than the act of living, and others interpret it as a piece of saintliness; he is remotely kind and dully tolerant, and behaves tranquilly, like a patient whose consciousness of his frightful pain is obscured by sedation. At last he is killed by a stupid vulgarian suffering from a crude and selfish delusion. It is not even a martyrdom.

This is Graham Greene at his best. He has a unique gift, which is not so much like the talent of a British or even an American author but rather like that of a suicidally disillusioned Frenchman, say Céline, or a God-seeking, God-deserted Russian. He can describe a man who is worthless and hopeless, doing things which are paltry, improbable, or contemptible in surroundings which are mean and colorless or foul and repellent; he can subtract all power and energy from the man's own personality, making him a mental and even a physical invalid—"a pair of ragged claws scuttling across the floors of silent seas"; he can play down the big moments of his story, so that they happen off stage and are only half realized even by the chief characters, who are too foolish or too brutal or too exhausted or too trivial to understand them fully; and yet, out of these unpromising materials and methods he can make a memorable novel, a durable symbol.

There is no politics in *A Burnt-Out Case,* apart from the coarse colonial who is a stereotype in every African novel nowadays. Most of the novel, and all its best chapters, are about personal suffering and one of its antidotes, religion. It is strange, but not after all inexplicable, that a man who writes so well about religious experience should write so badly about political experience.

Greene's work—by now a pretty large bookshelf—divides itself fairly clearly into books about crime, books about religion, and books about the shady side of international politics. The crime books, although skillful, are rather cheap and unrealistic. To write a really good book about crime one must be a detective, as Dashiell Hammett was for eight years, or spend many months working with the police and observing their patients and their methods, as Sidney Kingsley did, or at the very least, attend many trials and study the evidence of many more, as do criminologists such as F. Tennyson Jesse. There is no sign in Greene's crime books that he has ever done any of these things; and he is not quite a good enough psychologist to penetrate and interpret the minds of the vermin and lunatics who crowd our criminal courts.

His religious books are impressive. Their motto is that which many Christians have breathed and many pagans have groaned: "Lord, I believe: help thou mine unbelief." From time to time on late television one sees a revival of Greene's haunting story *The Power and the Glory,* about a priest hounded through Mexico during the antireligious years of the Revolution. The haggard face of Henry Fonda, the bare desecrated churches, the sad half-Indian believers slinking in to receive communion and to touch the representative of God, the vindictive police, and the cheap café life outside make an unforgettably pathetic scene: a disquieting and painful scene, because we know it is, even without blows, a war which will never be lost or won this side of eternity.

Perhaps he is at heart a Manichee, as St. Augustine was for many years of his life; perhaps he believes that mankind is the creation of the devil, living in a world which, when purified or liberated from the disease of humanity, will at last be good. Certainly he overstates the odds. There are other religious groups in the world hard at work, besides the Roman Catholics. Protestants, too, have their hospitals and their missions; Eastern Orthodox do many works of charity and service; the Jews spread their benevolence widely among their people; Buddhists and Mohammedans and many others do the work of God as they see it. This you would hardly grasp from Greene's novels, in which the Roman Catholic church is always the one, lonely, active, suffering minority, fighting against both the multitudes of barbarism and the human inadequacy of its own sons.

Manichaeism was never a very good solution to the moral problems of the universe. It is even less satisfactory when applied to politics. Our world, Greene appears to think, is the creation of a devil who was originally European and is now American. Everything vulgar, everything unjust, everything cheap and crude, everything oppressive—squawking radios, petty gangsters, mass-produced clothes, useless gadgets, the very lack of sympathy between individuals and groups—all this is built into Western society, which created it and lives on it. To destroy all these miseries, what must we do? Greene cannot tell; it is not the novelist's duty to tell. All he can say is that the miseries are European, Western European, and American —even more American—and that they are unutterably vile. Sometimes they are masterminded by rich fiends such as Krogh, the capitalist fraud modeled upon Ivar Kreuger in *England Made Me;* sometimes by poor and greedy devils such as the Orson Welles villain of *The Third Man,* who black-markets penicillin; sometimes, even worse, they are maintained and supported by a clean-limbed, healthy, naïve American, like the agent in *The Quiet American* who organizes a bombing in a Far Eastern city, to prove that there is a Third Force between the Communists and the far-right-wing military clique; but they are nearly always vile. No, sometimes they are ridiculous. In *Our Man in Havana* we are asked to believe that the British intelligence service is so disorganized and so shortsighted that it hires a bankrupt expatriate as its chief agent in Cuba and accepts his amateurish drawings of a vacuum cleaner as plans for a rocket launcher: the implication being generally that all secret service operations (at least on our side) are ridiculous and, incidentally, that there is no reason for anyone to worry about Cuba—where no rocket sites could possibly be built, or if built, could not be detected by us.

In 1957 Greene, together with a collaborator, published a book, which was partly amusing and partly exasperating, called *The Spy's Bedside Book.* It was a collection of extracts from stories of espionage and sabotage: some of them low-grade fiction (such as the rubbishy stories of William Le Queux), some of them weird and exaggerated memories (such as T. E. Lawrence's description of his sufferings under torture), some of them apparently real and factual; but all were so selected and so grouped as to convince the reader that all spies are as crazy as our man in Havana and that the entire business of espionage is worthless, like the art of telling the future from tarot cards, or else that it is a closed mystery behind which powerful and malevolent men manipulate the fortunes of a helpless humanity, themselves scarcely aware of the responsibilities they carry.

Perhaps Mr. Greene's experience of the modern world is limited by the difficulties of travel; he may be partially blinded by his own political strabismus; or, conceivably, he has not yet realized that although the Western world is in many ways "seedy" and in some respects corrupt, there exists another world far more grim, far less hospitable to the Christian religion, and far more contemptuous of human suffering. This is the world of communism, where the destinies of many hundreds of millions of human beings are controlled by a few thousand men much more intelligent and ruthless than any of Mr. Greene's own fictional creations. He likes visiting dismal places, where idealism meets reality and is beaten into the mud. I should like to propose that some Foundation (which would not object to being satirized later) finance an extended trip for him, first to Poland, where he can talk to the intellectuals who are caught in a desperately Manichaean trap, and then to some of the remoter leper colonies which exist in the Union of Soviet Socialist Republics: for example, Kolyma, far northeast in the Arctic Circle, where intellectuals and criminals and religious and dissentients work together in a hideous communion to dig gold out of the permanently frozen earth and wait for a release which depends on the whim of man—far more, apparently, than on the will of God.

—GILBERT HIGHET

ADVERTISING

No Deposit, No Return

The Affluent Society is a wonderful place, or thing, or notion, but to feel at home there it is well to have been born into it. Those of us who recall the Indigent Society of the thirties, or the more placid days before we even suspected we were any sort of Society at all, develop a kind of uneasiness when we are confronted with the A.S. in some of its more remarkable manifestations.

Consider, if you will, the latest method by which the Pepsi-Cola corporation plans to serve its public. Over the years Pepsi-Cola has made a pretty good thing out of bottling its product and moving it straightaway into the home. The corporation has also maintained the position that it is engaged in the sale of Pepsi-Cola, not of bottles, and consequently has expected to get the bottles back; to stimulate their return it has demanded a two-cent deposit on each bottle, which it refunded graciously when the bottle came home.

Recently, however, the company decided that this imposed too great a strain upon the faithful, and it is now providing a no-deposit bottle, which the customer may use to store bacon drippings, to fill with beetles, or simply to throw away. Naturally, one pays for this. In the New York area the no-deposit bottles, duly filled with Pepsi-Cola, will come a little high: sixty-seven cents for the six-pack. The regular deposit bottles cost only forty-nine cents plus twelve cents for the bottles.

The odd thing is that Pepsi-Cola gives you your choice, and if you look a little closely you will notice that by buying the deposit bottles and throwing *them* away, you will save six cents on the six-pack. It may seem morally indefensible to throw away six bottles that are worth twelve cents at the corner store, but we must face the fact that you save money that way, and to be frugal is the housewife's morality.

Perhaps we may expect the company to announce a further stride forward: the sale of no-deposit bottles *without* Pepsi-Cola. The purchaser can then take the six-pack home and throw it away immediately, without even the bother of opening the bottles and drinking the contents. This is about as convenient as you can get, but I hate to think how much they will have to charge for this.

It all may look great to Galbraith, but it strikes at the very roots of the economy with which I am familiar. The deposit bottle once meant everything to the growing child. Mothers were reluctant to part with cold cash, but they were rarely strong on the more general aspects of economic theory, and after a brief period of accumulation a pantry full of bottles looked more like a litter than an asset. At this point the youngster would be permitted to shoulder the load and move it back to the stores—usually half a dozen different stores, since shopkeepers redeemed only the bottles they had sold. This strengthened the kid's legs. In congested neighborhoods the existence of the deposit bottle also provided the child's first training in petty larceny, in preparation for a career in grand larceny, or merchandising, later in life.

If all this appears to be merely nostalgic, let it be noted that the deposit bottle, as a natural unit of currency, has never been matched for soundness and stability. So far as I know, no one ever defaulted on a deposit bottle—not in our neighborhood, anyway. I shall not derogate the bottle by saying that it was as good as gold, since it was far better than gold. Two cents for the small bottles and five cents for the large, and that is what it has been ever since I can remember. If this nation had ever had the good sense to go on the deposit-bottle standard, Coolidge would probably still be president, and you couldn't ask for more than that.

Well, convenience is now the cry (not that Coolidge wasn't convenient when it suited his purposes), and we mustn't swim against the current. It is costly, but money is what we have most of. A friend of mine defined the Affluent Society as one in which it is more irritating to spend money than to earn it, and he may be right. Supermarkets now offer charcoal prepackaged for outdoor grills; it comes neatly embedded, cube by cube, in a specially treated box which serves also as kindling and is impregnated with something or other so that it bursts into flame at a heated remark. In this form the charcoal costs about $72,000 a ton (I calculated this on my fingers, of which I have very few, and may be out by sixty or seventy thousand dollars).

It would be pleasant to believe that all this affluence buys us more than no-deposit bottles at a substantial markup. This brings to mind the remark of a most estimable gentleman whom I chanced to accompany on his first visit to Chartres. Overcome by the sight, he said, "It's a pity, but it has to be faced: we couldn't build anything like this any more. We couldn't even attempt to. We are much too rich." He was absolutely right, beyond the possibility of argument. All that the Affluent Society can afford are things to throw away, shoot away, or to consume joylessly, in a great hurry.

—STEPHEN WHITE

JASPER JOHNS

drawings & sculptures
lithographs

JAN. 31-FEB. 18

LEO CASTELLI 4 E 77

Upon receiving the above announcement from the Leo Castelli gallery, the editors visited the exhibition of works by the young American artist Jasper Johns. There it became clear that Mr. Johns was not exhibiting two beer cans but two meticulously cast and finished bronze sculptures, painted to resemble beer cans. One can has been "opened" and is relatively light; the other, unopened and heavy, is apparently full. With studies of his more familiar flags, numerals, and targets, the artist exhibited several other bronze sculptures: a light bulb, light bulb with cord and socket, a flashlight, and seventeen paint brushes in a coffee tin (both tin and brushes painted so as to be indistinguishable from the appurtenances of a studio). Of forty-five works, only three went unsold; *Two Beer Cans* was sold for $1,200 to Mr. and Mrs. Robert Scull of Great Neck, Long Island.

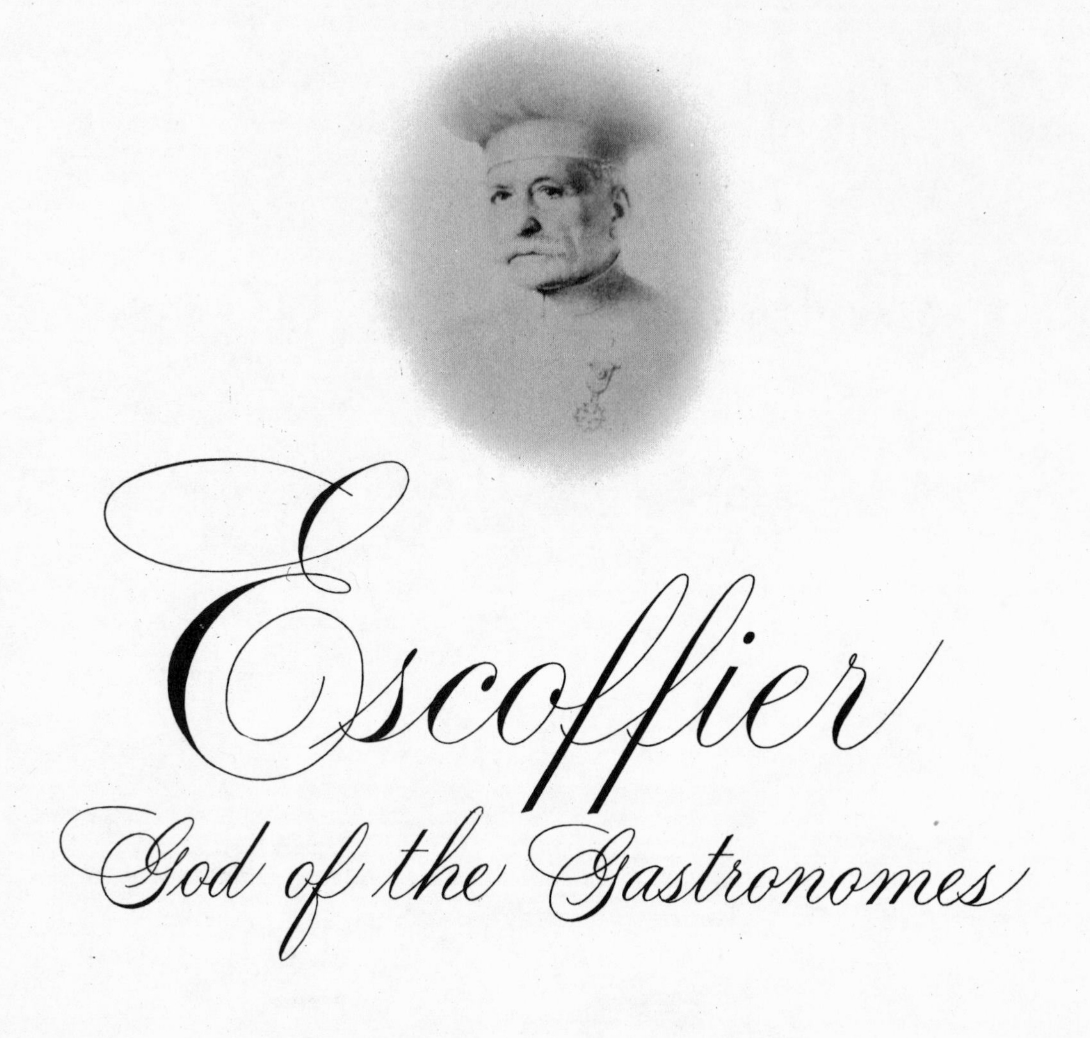

Escoffier: God of the Gastronomes

One evening around the turn of the century the Prince of Wales (later Edward VII) appeared for dinner at London's elegant Savoy Hotel, where his attention was arrested by an intriguing item toward the top of the menu. *"Cuisses de Nymphes à l'Aurore,"* it read—Nymphs' Thighs at Dawn. This was clearly a case of *noblesse oblige,* and the Prince obliged by ordering it. The dish was presented; the Prince nibbled reflectively; then, puzzled, he called for the chef and demanded to know what he was eating. Frogs' legs, announced the chef with a low bow. (In this case poached in a white-wine *court-bouillon,* steeped in a fragrant cream and fish sauce, spiced with paprika, tinted gold, covered with a champagne aspic-jelly to imitate water, and served cold.)

In those days the British upper crust regarded the lowly frog as too vulgar an animal to merit gastronomic obeisance, and so the ingenious chef who had supplied the mythological disguise waited uncertainly for the royal verdict. Delicious, pronounced the Prince. And another unpalatable English prejudice was swept into the dustbin of history. From that evening onward, Nymphs' Thighs were offered to the best people in the best London restaurants, and the chef became renowned as the man who taught the English to eat frogs.

He was, of course, a Frenchman. He was also a genius. He was Georges Auguste Escoffier (1846–1935), famed as "the king of chefs and the chef of kings." Kings and queens, emperors and empresses, kaisers and czars reigned throughout Europe in the aristocratic days when Escoffier began as a scullery boy and started on his vertiginous and revolutionary career as perhaps the greatest culinary artist ever to preside over a hot stove; and most of these monarchs—from Napoleon III and Queen Victoria to the equally regal and more numerous rulers of Scandinavia and the Balkans—partook of his sumptuously delicate creations. He plied George V with innumerable variations of the monarch's favorite dish, cream cheese, demonstrating that even so plebeian a theme could be rendered noble. On one notable occasion, aboard the Hamburg-Amerika liner *Imperator,* later the *Berengaria,* he fed Kaiser Wilhelm so superbly with salmon steamed in champagne that after the banquet the German ruler congratulated him effusively and is reputed to have asked, "How can I repay you?" "By giving us back Alsace-Lorraine," the Frenchman replied. It was the last time Escoffier cooked for the Kaiser.

Being the chef of kings may be prestigious, but it is as the

By BERNARD FRIZELL

king of chefs that Escoffier achieved his undisputed and greater glory. If experts were asked to name the greatest poet, painter, novelist, playwright, or composer of the twentieth century, it is most improbable that in any instance they would agree. They are unanimous, however, on Escoffier as the century's finest practitioner of civilization's most underrated and only indispensable art—cooking.

It is not for his cooking alone, remarkable as it was, that Escoffier is renowned. He did, of course, possess to a supreme degree the gift of knowing how to devise original flavors and mingle familiar ones into novel taste sensations, exercising that gift with the flair of a painter enriching his palette; and his repertoire was said to include ten thousand recipes, many of which bore the genial Escoffier signature. "A sauce," he said, "must fit the roast or fish as closely as a tight-fitting skirt fits a woman," and he tailored his sauces accordingly. The most famous of his creations was invented by the enthralled chef when he returned to the tranquillity of his kitchen after hearing Nellie Melba sing Elsa in *Lohengrin* and in a moment of inspiration immortalized the diva for gourmets. *Pêche Melba,* though all too often desecrated by counterfeit versions, is a little masterpiece of well-calculated simplicity that has stood the test of time. (Escoffier's laconic directions: poach the peaches in vanilla-flavored syrup. Put them in a *timbale* upon a layer of vanilla ice cream, and coat them with raspberry purée. The raspberry purée was, of course, the master stroke.) Less well known, but not less good for that, is another simple but seductive dessert, *Baisers de Vierge*—Virgin's Kisses—a light, fragrant whiff of taste consisting of meringue and whipped cream mixed with crystallized white violets and white rose petals and served with an apricot sauce perfumed with kirsch. "These innocent little virgin's kisses," ran Escoffier's Gallic comment, "will no doubt later become flowers of sin."

Nonetheless, behind the hand that executed these chefs-d'oeuvre was a mind informed by the ambition to do more than merely sound isolated chords of exquisite taste. Escoffier's high purpose in the realm of taste was nothing less than symphonic. His seminal insight was that, like music, the grand structure of gastronomy is built upon the harmony and sequence of its elements. Indeed his imagery, in the unveiling of his thought, was musical. "After the manner of an overture in a light opera," he wrote, "soup should divulge what is to be the dominant phrase of the melody throughout." His score was the menu, and the composition of menus he considered to be "among the most difficult problems of our art, and it is in this very matter that perfection is so rarely reached."

If, then, Escoffier was *hors concours* as a chef in our times, it was no more for the virtuosity with which he manipulated a skillet than for the grand conception of eating that he developed and imposed. He contemplated the problem profoundly; it is no exaggeration to say that he contemplated it philosophically, probing its basic concepts. His analysis and rejection of the floury and indigestible basic sauces of his time were incisive and revolutionary. Escoffier, in the words of André L. Simon, the British connoisseur, "had what may be considered the audacity to denounce the two traditional basic sauces of French cuisine, *l'Espagnole* and *l'Allemande,* both old-fashioned French sauces in spite of their names, the first a sauce *brune* and the other a sauce *blonde*. He substituted for them and their numerous bastard progeny the much lighter and more fragrant *fumets,* the concentrated natural juices of meat, fish and vegetables in water, broth, butter, olive oil or any other cooking media."

That was not all. Having altered the substructure of his art in the interests of taste and digestibility, Escoffier proceeded to refashion its superstructure by developing an original aesthetic of the table. He conceived each dish in any meal as an individual work of art that fitted, like the movements of a quartet or symphony, in a precise order and scale of values into the larger scheme of a greater work of art, the meal itself as defined by the menu. This concept is so fundamental to his philosophy of food, its fabrication and consumption, that as an indispensable accompaniment to his cardinal opus, *Le Guide Culinaire (The Escoffier Cook Book),* in which he incorporated 2,973 of his recipes, he wrote the equally basic work, *Le Livre des Menus,* in which he composed dazzling combinations of many of those recipes to explore varied and unexpected adventures in tastes.

The originality of Escoffier's concept can best be appreciated against the culinary tradition out of which he sprang. It was totally different from the one he handed down to succeeding generations. In the beginning of the nineteenth century in France the mere notion of a sequence of tastes, where it existed at all, had little refinement. Soup, for example, as we know it today, is a relatively recent innovation and had barely made its appearance on the gastronomic scene. *La soupe* of old France—still a tasty if crude dish to linger over in the peasant backwaters of the provinces—was a meal in itself, with the meats and vegetables used in its preparation all thrown together and eaten at once. This was not untypical of the confused and rather primitive menu in those days. "These menus," Escoffier wrote, "seem to have depended in no wise, for their items, upon the progressive satisfaction of the diners' appetites, and a long procession of dishes was far more characteristic of the meal than their judicious order and diversity."

In his mild way Escoffier understated the case. For in those days of lavish splendor and culinary excess each part of the meal consisted of a multiplicity of different dishes of more or less the same category, and all of them were served simultaneously. When the guests entered the dining room, there for the delectation of all eyes was the table fully loaded. It was generally a table of ample dimensions, and it groaned, depending upon the number of guests and the ingenuity of the chef, under the weight of forty, fifty, or even a hundred different dishes. The sight was spectacular—

though the food might not be very hot—and the ah's and oh's it elicited made a memorable moment. For the gastronomic spirit of the time, with its immense architectural cakes, its sugared arabesques, its *grosses pièces* of fish, beef, pig, and lamb, its icing-sculptured pastries, demanded a spectacle for the eye as a condition for the satisfaction of the taste.

The dominant personality in the art of cooking in those distant days was the immortal Marie-Antoine Carême, a man of taste, discrimination, stature, and genius. He recognized that cooking is the oldest of the arts (". . . for Adam was born hungry") and that he was an artist. As such, he regarded his work as apostolic and was uncompromising toward those who failed to meet his rigorous critical standards. Recalling feasts composed of forty-eight entrees that he helped prepare for Talleyrand, he wrote in his three-volume masterpiece, *Le Maître d'Hôtel Français,* "These great dinners recalled the ancient glory of French cooking." The remark is an indication that he was not only dissatisfied with the general state of the cookery of his day but that he favored the gastronomic opulence of the *ancien régime.* It was Carême who in his vigorous and polemical style began the critique of French cooking, particularly as to the order and variety of the menu, that Escoffier in his gentler manner was to complete. Carême was especially violent against those chefs who with stunning virtuosity prepared feasts for their aristocratic patrons consisting of perhaps forty brilliant variations on a solitary theme, like pig or beef or lamb. In short, Carême, a virtuoso himself, took a position of unshakable principle against virtuosity for virtuosity's sake.

He remained, however, within the general culinary philosophy of his day. The menu of a luncheon he prepared for forty guests of the Prince Regent at Brighton in January, 1817, required three closely printed pages, almost all of them double-columned. This luncheon, which must have left the lucky forty sated (perhaps for days), encompassed one hundred and twenty-four different dishes beginning with eight soups (*la tortue au vin de Madère, la croûte gratiné au céleri,* etc.) and ending with *petits soufflés à l'orange* and *fondue au Parmesan.* In between, to tantalize the taste buds and meet the imperious demands of appetite, there were eight different preparations of fish (*le turbot grillé, sauce aux huîtres; le saumon à la Génoise,* etc.), eight little "nibbles" between the fish and the entrees (a quarter of a kid, suckling pig, etc.), forty-two entrees (*le turban de filets mignons à l'écarlate, les pigeons innocents à la cuillère, de petits soufflés de volaille et de gibier, le pain de foies gras à la gelée,* etc.), eight plates of roasts (barded quails, pheasants, chickens, etc.), forty entremets (*les truffes à l'Italienne, les oeufs à la Bretonne, les crèmes françaises au café moka, les tartelettes glacées aux pistaches,* etc.), and around the table, to be admired, demolished, and consumed, eight architectured spectaculars built of lobster, turkey, ham, etc.

It was copious. It was opulent. It was also gross. No doubt each dish was a treasure; but with each multitudinous-dished course being served at once, the effect could not but be disorderly. What any guest ate, moreover, must have been in some measure a matter of chance, with the probability high that none tasted all one hundred and twenty-four of the delicacies Carême masterminded that January day. If the *côtelettes de moutons à la Soubise* and the *escalopes de faisans aux truffes de France* happened to have been at the opposite end of the table, then no matter how much the guest liked mutton chops with a butter, onion, and cream sauce, or black-truffled slices of pheasant, he might have had to content himself with the regal pot luck of *les filets de canards sauvages à la bigarade* and *le sauté de bécasses, sauce salmis,* persuading himself all the way home, no doubt, that having eaten, among other things, a Carême preparation of wild duck with orange sauce and sautéed woodcock with a sauce made of red wine, shallots, and the bird's minced intestines, the day could not be considered a total loss.

And yet, despite his great predecessor's clash of cymbals and blare of trumpets, Escoffier recalled that the Prince Regent had assured Carême during his stay at the English court that his cooking was the only cooking his Highness had found at all easy to digest. Escoffier generously commented, "Carême had grasped the essential truth that the richer cooking is, the more speedily do the stomach and palate tire of it." In any event, not until the middle of the nineteenth century did *le service à la française,* the simultaneous presentation of a multiplicity of dishes, begin to be replaced by an import from Russia, *le service à la russe,* the presentation of individual dishes in sequence as we know it today.

It was at this point in the history of French gastronomy that Georges Auguste Escoffier made his modest appearance on the scene. He was born in the sun-drenched Provençal hilltop village of Villeneuve-Loubet, not far from Antibes, the son of a jovial blacksmith, who made more money marketing his tobacco plants than shoeing horses. The practical old man was unimpressed with his son's talent for drawing and desire to become a painter (good enough for leisure but not for a living), and when the boy was thirteen insisted that he learn a trade. So father took son out of school and to Nice, where the old man's brother had opened Le Restaurant Français, a fine establishment that remained in existence more than fifty years, catering to a rich foreign clientele. There little Georges Auguste began his apprenticeship. His uncle taught him well. In five years the diminutive youngster learned the business from the most menial tasks in the kitchen to the purchase of provisions and the organization of the service. By that time he came upon a double professional conviction he never lost: "To know how to eat is to know how to live," and "No man should have less than two hours for the chief meal of the day." "Good cooking," he was later to write with extraordinary faith in his art, "is the foundation of true happiness."

To become a master of that art, Escoffier knew he had to

*The florid menu card is no new invention, but during Escoffier's time—unlike today—the food usually lived up to the salesmanship. The cards above call attention to some of his specialties with fanciful but rather heavy-handed illustrations (*canard en chemise *is represented by a duck in a slip). The one below, with many references to the royal family in both art work and menu, celebrates the coronation of King George V.*

-- DINER DE GALA --

Hors d'Œuvre Moscovite
Melon Cantaloup

Tortue Claire
Velouté de Volaille Froid

Mousseline de Truite aux Ecrevisses

Poularde Georges V

Selle d'Agneau de Galles
Petits Pois à l'Anglaise

Suprêmes de Caneton à la Gelée au Porto

Cailles aux Raisins
Salade Orientale

Cœurs d'Artichauts Grand Duc

Pêches Reine Mary
Mignardises

Fruits

Carlton Hôtel & Restaurant.

Jeudi, 22 Juin, 1911.

COLLECTION OF JOSEPH DONON

COLLECTION OF DR. J. B. ESCOFFIER

La Pêche Melba
son Origine.

Madame Nellie Melba, grande Cantatrice, de nationalité Australienne, chantait a Covent Garden à Londres, avec Jean de Reské en 1894, elle habitait le Savoy Hôtel près de Covent Garden, époque ou je dirigeais les cuisines de cet important établissement. Un soir ou l'on donnait Lohengrin, Madame Melba m'offrit deux fauteuils d'orchestre. On sait que, dans cet Opéra il apparait un Cygne. Madame Melba, donnait le lendemain soir un petit souper à quelques intimes dont Monseigneur le Duc d'Orléans était parmi les convives; et pour lui montrer que j'avais agréablement profité des fauteuil qu'elle m'avait gracieusement offerts, je fis tailler, dans un bloc de glace un superbe Cygne, et, entre les deux ailes j'incrustai une timbale en argent. Je couvrai le fond de la timbale de glace à la vanille et sur ce lit de fine glace je disposai des pêches, à chair blanche et tendre et débarassées de leur pelure, puis pochées pendant quelques minutes dans un sirop à la vanille et refroidies. Une purée de framboises fraîches couvrant complètement les pêches, (un léger voile en sucre filé jettais sur les pêches) complétait délicieusement cet entremets devenu mondial.

Mais, ce n'est qu'en 1899 à l'ouverture du Carlton à Londres que la Pêche Melba a conquis sa popularité.

Dans le service courant, la "Pêche Melba" est le dessert le plus facile à préparer, il suffit de couvrir le fond d'une coupe en cristal d'un lit de fine glace a la vanille, déposer sur la glace des pêches à chair blanche et tendre, mûres à point, débarassées de leur pelure, pochées pendant quelques minutes dans un sirop léger parfumé à la vanille. Puis masquer les pêches d'une purée de framboises fraîches, sucrée.

Facultativement on peut jetter sur les pêches, un léger voile en sucre filé.

A. Escoffier

Pêche Melba is Escoffier's most popular creation, although what passes for it in the average restaurant is a travesty of the real thing. At right is his own account of how he invented it in 1894, after Dame Nellie Melba (below) had given him two tickets to Lohengrin, *along with his own instructions for making it (page 121). Even when they are followed to the letter, the result is not universally admired—as the dissent below makes abundantly clear.*

CULVER PICTURES, INC.

Pêche Melba: A Dissent

The *Pêche Melba* is typical of much of Escoffier's cuisine—garish, colorful, vulgar: easily mass-produced yet giving the illusion of a rare delicacy and then dedicated to a world figure to ensure its publicity. Most of Escoffier's names for his dishes make a gourmet wince, and his blend of overemphatic flavors outrage the palate by their insistence on the obvious. *Pêche Melba* is derived from the classical cuisine. The true dish is this: fresh peaches bathed in a syrup made from the juice of other peaches to which a sufficient sugar has been added and then reduced. About half an hour before serving, whilst the fruit is being lightly chilled, the juice of fresh raspberries should be added to the syrup, enough to tinge the syrup, not sufficient to dye it, pink. This, with fresh cream, is the best accompaniment for the finest sauternes. Escoffier has taken this blend of flavors, frozen the cream, stuck on the peach, and covered it with a raspberry syrup that hits the palate with the violence of a pickled onion. What could one drink with such a dish? *Only* ice water.

—J. H. Plumb

go to the school of Paris. Off he went to the capital in the spring of 1865 to work as *commis-rôtisseur* in the fashionable Restaurant du Petit Moulin Rouge under Ulysse Rohan, a talented but temperamental chef. Wearing high heels to put that much more distance between his head and the heat of the ovens, little Escoffier learned the hard way under Rohan's brutal discipline. But he persisted, and when the Franco-Prussian War broke out in 1870 and Escoffier was called to the colors, he had achieved the proud eminence of sauce chef.

Not even war could stay the headlong pace of the dedicated youth's culinary education. As an army chef during the siege of Metz, he learned how to cook a horse (scald the meat and cool before cooking to kill the bitter taste) and later wrote of those days of defeat, "Horse-meat is delicious when one is in the right circumstances to appreciate it." He was of course able to make do with truffles when potatoes proved harder to find, and his *lapin sauté,* improvised in the heat of a campaign, was not calculated to displease the officers who ate it (cut the rabbit in pieces and brown in hot lard; add six finely chopped large onions, pepper and salt; pour on a glass of cognac and the same amount of white wine and let it simmer for twenty minutes; then serve). But his most embattled wartime experience came one night in a Homeric scene when the rudimentary spit upon which he had hoisted an enormous joint of beef blazed with light and he was forced to draw his sword and defend the animal from the attacks of impatient Zouaves.

After the war Escoffier perfected his style. He became head chef of the Petit Moulin Rouge, then with extreme brilliance guided the culinary destinies of a number of other outstanding establishments in Paris and on the Côte d'Azur. But though his reputation was growing within the profession, he was still relatively unknown. A large question now loomed, a question of ultimates that depended to some degree on chance. Escoffier was not yet out of his thirties, but he had come head-on to the critical point in his career. Would he stand still at his considerable level of excellence, or would he climb to the peak of his art and achieve universal renown? A chef, like an actor, requires an opportunity for greatness. He cannot achieve it in a small kitchen and with limited means. He must be given a stage and a free hand. Only then, if he truly has greatness in him, can he stretch to his full height. The occasion for greatness came to Escoffier in the Riviera season of 1883–84 when he fatefully met another relative unknown, the fast-rising hotelier César Ritz, whose name, for its association with impeccable elegance, had not yet become a part of the language.

Before anyone ever thought of putting on the ritz, Ritz put on Escoffier—as the guiding luminary of the kitchens and dining rooms of the Grand Hotel in Monte Carlo. César Ritz, well in advance of his time, believed that a hotel was no better than its cuisine. He soon came to the thoughtful and well-observed conclusion that "Monsieur Escoffier is undoubtedly the finest chef in the world."

It was the beginning of a long association that was to bring fame to both men and spread the cult of the classic French cuisine to the far corners of the gastronomic world. Already in Monte Carlo, as Ritz happily acceded to his young chef's revolutionary ideas, princes of the blood, British, Swedish, and Lithuanian; Grand Dukes of Russia and Spain; South American millionaires; Oriental potentates; kings of American industry and finance; and Europe's theatrical aristocracy led by Sarah Bernhardt, Coquelin, and D'Oyly Carte were flocking to Escoffier's table to savor and applaud his inventions. While admitting that "a cook's first duty is to conform to the desires of amphytrions and customers," Escoffier remorselessly prepared his campaign against the bad taste of the day. He was already fighting his intrepid battle against that grotesque gastronomic fixture, the *sorbet,* a highly perfumed ice served midway through the meal, which disappeared from his later and more mature menus. He followed Brillat-Savarin's rule, "The order of food in a dinner is from the more substantial to the lighter," for "the appetite is appeased in eating." And he insisted on the principle, then avant-garde, now a truism, that a man should "rise from table having precisely satisfied his appetite without overcharging the stomach."

The man who in humility was to write, "It would be absurd to aspire to fix the destinies of an art," was now ready to play his most glorified role. With Ritz he went to London in 1890 where his stage was the Savoy, and then the Carlton Hotel, with a brief interlude between the two at the Paris Ritz. His means were unlimited. His public was the richest, most aristocratic, and most fastidious in the world. Escoffier rose to the challenge and cooked his way to fame. "The Savoy of London," wrote one contemporary observer, "became the sacrosanct meeting place of international aristocracy, an oasis for artists, the mecca of gourmets and a goal of pilgrimages from the five parts of the world."

Success did not turn the head of the little man with the shaggy white mustache and bright eyes, who wore a high white chef's hat in the kitchen, but changed to impeccable striped trousers and a Louis-Philippe dress coat to welcome the mighty in the dining room. He remained courteous, modest, soft-spoken, and imperturbable even in the most exasperating crises—a quality rare in cooks, whose chief emotion at work is often, and understandably so, anxiety. When pushed beyond endurance by some grotesque error, his left hand would go to his face; he would rub his cheek, seize his ear with two fingers, then manfully leave the kitchen, murmuring, "I'm going out; I can feel myself getting angry."

In London, brigades of sixty to eighty cooks worked under this gentle man who never had to raise his voice to impose discipline. From his kitchen, as from a school, hundreds of Escoffier-trained cooks emerged to work on luxury liners and in the great hotels and restaurants of the world's capitals, practicing and preaching the doctrine of the master and sowing the seed of his theory. The result was that all around the world, from the Transvaal to Russia, from the two Americas to Egypt, French cooking of the Escoffier school became a standard. His reforms, down to organization, were radical. In the kitchen chaos of the old regime, for example, one cook took fifteen minutes to prepare eggs Meyerbeer. Under Escoffier's system of specialists, an *entremettier* baked the eggs; a *rôtisseur* grilled the kidneys; a *saucier* whipped up the truffle sauce, and a gourmet was rendered ecstatic in only a few minutes.

Escoffier retired in 1919 at seventy-three and let his wife do the cooking ("She cooks far better than I do") until he died in his native Provence in his eighty-ninth year. Only one full serving of Escoffier has been offered in book form—a biography by two disciples, Eugène Herbodeau and Paul Thalamas. They may be better at mixing a sauce than pushing a pen, but they understood Escoffier and his historic role in the art that most of us, for better or worse, are exposed to three times a day. Out of a tradition in which a dinner might last a marathon eighteen hours, as did those famed Saturday feasts of the *Club des Grands Estomacs,* Escoffier forged a new concept, replacing Gargantuan plenitude and baroque splendor with classic simplicity. He was as capable as any man of displaying the dazzling pyrotechnics of the French *haute cuisine,* but his answer to Carême's extravagance was that simplicity which first disarms, then proves stunning. The simple dishes in the Escoffier tradition? They are such familiar offerings as *truite à la meunière* (after the trout is dipped in flour, it is sautéed in butter and served with a sauce of the butter it cooked in, plus a little lemon juice and chopped parsley), *tournedos Rossini* (the cut of steak is cooked *au point* and served with *foie gras* and a slice of truffle on top of it and a little sauce made with the juice of the cooked meat and some Madeira wine), *suprêmes de volaille Jeannette* (the chicken breasts are boiled and an aspic-jelly perfumed with tarragon is made from the broth and poured on the chicken, which is served cold with slices of *foie gras*).

This simplicity (and its accompanying subtlety) was extended to the larger area of Escoffier's art. He handled flavors as a musician handles sounds, and his menus were like chamber music in their gradation of tastes. In 1912 he prepared a royal dinner at the Carlton for Spain's Alfonso XIII; the menu consisted of a bare seven courses—an immense descent, and leap, from Carême's banquets. The dinner, typical Escoffier, opened that August night on the fresh, sweet note of melon, modulated to the more subtle tone of *petite marmite à la moëlle* (a beef consommé made with carrots, turnips, leeks, and celery), sounded a lush chord with *sole Tosca* (the sauce for the sole is made of cream, white wine, shallots, and little white grapes), then hit two consecutive and very different notes of brass and woodwind in the *selle d'agneau de Galles* (a roast saddle of lamb served with braised lettuce) and a *poularde de Bresse à la broche* (chicken roasted on a spit over charcoal and served with a salad). Then came the resolution in *aubergines à l'Orientale* (eggplant and rice with pimento and tomato) and a light dessert of vanilla ice cream and biscuits and fresh peaches and raspberries.

Words cannot, of course, convey tastes, and neither prose nor poetry can do justice to Escoffier's creations—they are untranslatable. His style was deceptive, really the most difficult of all. Because it was simple French cooking, true French cooking, and it demanded what he aimed at—perfection. For in its delicacy of balance a miss by so much as an eyelash was always apt to result in total disaster.

Tastes are transitory, however; and since a chef's masterpieces, unlike those of other artists, are short-lived, Escoffier's bid for immortality lies in his major literary effort, *Le Guide Culinaire,* in which he codified the classic French cuisine by reducing guesswork descriptions to measurable formulas. In the opinion of his biographers it represented "the sum total of the secrets amassed by the old masters" and ended the age of empiricism in the kitchen. With *Le Livre des Menus* they consider it "a testament of the most outstanding epoch in the evolution of the art of cookery." Escoffier characteristically claimed much less for his weighty volume. He described it as "a thesaurus of selected recipes and not a complete formulary." Its thousands of recipes include 213 soups, 143 egg dishes, and 189 ways to make chicken taste enchanting; in between, it ranges from the definition of an omelette ("scrambled eggs enclosed in a coating of coagulated egg") to instructions on how to slaughter a turtle ("Lay it on its back on a table with its head hanging over the side. By means of a double butcher's hook, one spike of which is thrust into the turtle's lower jaw, while the other suspends an adequately heavy weight, make the animal hold its head back; then, quickly as possible, sever the head from the body").

There is no doubt that in range and subtlety, French cooking is the best in the world or that Escoffier takes his place beside France's most celebrated gastronomic personalities. He lacked the ornate glamour of Carême but surpassed him in austere art. He lacked the wit of Brillat-Savarin, but Brillat-Savarin was more gourmet than cook. He lacked the temperament of the great seventeenth-century chef, Vatel, but was more imaginative. Vatel committed suicide, impaling himself on a kitchen knife when the sole did not arrive in time for a dinner for Louis XIV. Asked what he would have done in Vatel's place, Escoffier did not hesitate. "I would have taken the white meat of chickens—very young chickens," he said, "and I would have made fillets of sole with them. No one would ever have known the difference."

As the Roving Correspondent in Europe for NBC News, Bernard Frizell makes his headquarters in Paris—and thus is fortunately situated to continue his researches in gastronomy. He has written two novels, Julie *and* Ten Days in August.

These formidable dishes were prepared for special occasions—the one at the left to honor Charles Nungesser and François Coli on the eve of their ill-fated transatlantic flight in 1927, the one below (concealing langouste glacée*) for the Fourth of July.*

Quant on voit un Restaurant à la Mode, comme tel restaurant de la rue Saint-Honoré, être contraint de faire figurer dans ses menus des chats des rats, on peut s'imaginer ce que sont les repas ordinaires en temps de siège.

Menu de Noël du Café Voisin
25 Décembre 1870
99me jour du Siège de Paris

Hors d'Œuvre
Beurre, Radis. Tête d'Âne farcie, Sardines
Potages
Soupe à la Purée de haricots rouges aux croûtons
Consommé d'Eléphant

Poissons et Entrées
Goujons Frits
Longe de Chameau ~~rôtie~~ à l'Anglaise
Kanguroo de conserve sauce piquante
Rôts
Cuissot de Loup sauce Chasseur
Plat d'antilope aux truffes
Chat accompagné de rats
Salade de Cresson
Petits pois paysanne
Champignons blancs à la Provençale
sautés à l'huile avec pointes d'ail
sel et poivre.

Entremets
Gâteau de riz et confitures
Dessert
Fromage de Gruyère

— 1916 — En considérant les choses en ce moment au point de vue de l'alimentation, on se refuserait de croire que l'Angleterre est en guerre car bien que les prix soient élevés la pénurie des denrées ne se fait pas encore trop sentir, ni par la qualité ni la quantité

In 1916 young French cooks were complaining that wartime food shortages made the haute cuisine *impossible. Escoffier urged them to rise to the occasion, as chefs had done during the much greater privations of the Franco-Prussian War. And as inspiration he recalled and wrote down the Christmas menu of the Café Voisin in 1870, on the ninety-ninth day of the siege of Paris. This meal—which must have challenged the diner even more than the cook—included elephant consommé, loin of camel* à l'Anglaise, *tinned kangaroo with* sauce piquante, *haunch of wolf with* sauce chasseur, *and (this sounds better untranslated)* chat accompagné de rats. *Except for the last, these exotic specialties were former residents of the Paris zoo.*

COLLECTION OF DR. J. B. ESCOFFIER

COLLECTION OF DR. J. B. ESCOFFIER

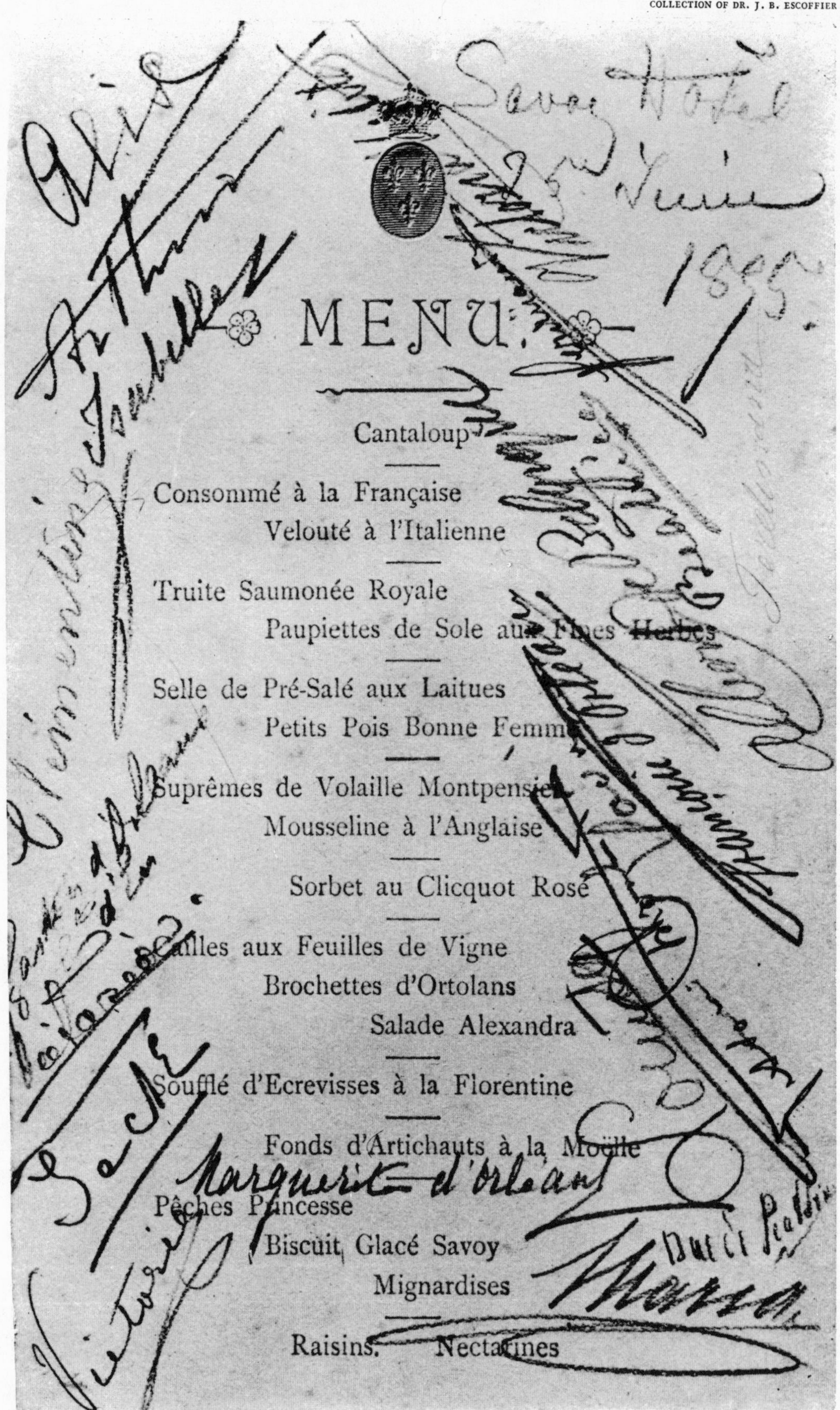

MENU

Cantaloup

Consommé à la Française
Velouté à l'Italienne

Truite Saumonée Royale
Paupiettes de Sole aux Fines Herbes

Selle de Pré-Salé aux Laitues
Petits Pois Bonne Femme

Suprêmes de Volaille Montpensier
Mousseline à l'Anglaise

Sorbet au Clicquot Rosé

Cailles aux Feuilles de Vigne
Brochettes d'Ortolans
Salade Alexandra

Soufflé d'Ecrevisses à la Florentine

Fonds d'Artichauts à la Moëlle

Pêches Princesse
Biscuit Glacé Savoy
Mignardises

Raisins. Nectarines

An imposing array of royal guests autographed Escoffier's menu for the wedding reception of the Duke of Aosta and Princess Hélène d'Orléans in 1895. Among the signers are Arthur (upper left), Duke of Connaught and seventh child of Queen Victoria; Albert de Belgique (middle right), later King Albert I of Belgium; and Princess Beatrice (next to Albert), Victoria's ninth child.